COPING WITH THE MASS MEDIA

JOSEPH F. LITTELL EDITOR

COPING WITH THE MASS MEDIA

McDOUGAL LITTELL
& COMPANY, EVANSTON, ILLINOIS

distributed to colleges and universities by
Canfield Press
A Department of Harper & Row, Publishers, Inc.
San Francisco

EDITORIAL DIRECTION: **JOY LITTELL**

EDITOR: **CLAUDIA NORLIN**

CONSULTANT: **BERGEN EVANS**

DESIGN: **WILLIAM A. SEABRIGHT**

EDITOR, STUDENT'S GUIDE: CLAUDIA NORLIN

CONTRIBUTORS: DAVID COYNIK, J. A. CHRISTENSEN

HN
90
.M3
C66
1976
c.2

Acknowledgments: See page 232.

ISBN 0–88343–302–8

Contents

THE ROLE OF THE MASS MEDIA 1

THE MASS MEDIA   STUART CHASE   **2**

THE MASS MEDIA AS "LANGUAGES"   ROY A. GALLANT   **5**

THE MASS MEDIA—A BALANCE SHEET   STUART CHASE   **11**

TELEVISION 15

TV OR NOT TV   **16**

A NATION OF VIDEOTS   AN INTERVIEW WITH JERZY KOSINSKI   **19**

WHAT TV IS DOING TO AMERICA
AN INTERVIEW WITH ALISTAIR COOKE   **27**

VIOLENCE ON TELEVISION   **36**

HOW TO TELL GOOD GUYS FROM BAD GUYS   JOHN STEINBECK   **39**

THE "LATE SHOW" CLICHE MOVIE SCRIPTS

THE "SWASHBUCKLER" MOVIE   **43**

THE "POLITICAL" MOVIE   **47**

THE "SOCIETY" MOVIE   **51**

HOW TO TALK BACK TO YOUR TV SET   NICHOLAS JOHNSON   **55**

HAVE THE TV NETWORKS GONE TOO FAR?
NICHOLAS JOHNSON, WHITNEY M. YOUNG, JR., FRANK STANTON   **63**

TV INTERVIEWS   HERBERT MITGANG   **65**

RADIO 67

RADIO, THE PARENT REBORN   LES BROWN   **69**

NEWSPAPERS 75

FINDING YOUR WAY THROUGH THE NEWSPAPER   77

WORKING NEWSMAN REVEALS HOW NEWSPAPERS ARE PUT TOGETHER
BEN H. BAGDIKIAN   83

HUMOR IN THE HEADLINES   96

INTERPRETING THE NEWS   100

ADVERTISING 103

ADVERTISING THROUGH THE MASS MEDIA   MAX BRAITHWAITE   105

UNDERSTANDING THE ADS   DAVID AND MARYMAE KLEIN   107

FOUR ADS FOR DISCUSSION   112

FEATURE-BY-FEATURE ADVERTISING   116

CAN ADVERTISERS BACK UP THEIR CLAIMS?   *CHANGING TIMES*   121

ADVERTISING PORTRAYING OR DIRECTED TO WOMEN
ADVERTISING AGE   125

NOTHING PERSONAL   JAMES BALDWIN   130

MOVIES 133

THE CAMERA AND THE AUDIENCE   GILBERT SELDES   135

THE NEW MOVIES   *NEWSWEEK*   141

THE FUTURE OF HOLLYWOOD   *SATURDAY REVIEW*   147

HOLLYWOOD'S MAVERICKS   HOLLIS ALPERT   151

REEL ONE   ADRIEN STOUTENBURG   155

TRASH, ART AND THE MOVIES   PAULINE KAEL   157

HAVE THE MOVIES GONE TOO FAR?   JUDITH CRIST,
THE CHICAGO TRIBUNE, BERGEN EVANS, JACK VALENTI   171

A NEW UNDERSTANDING OF MEDIA 173

THE NEW LANGUAGES   MARSHALL McLUHAN AND
EDMUND CARPENTER   **174**

THE MEDIA   MARSHALL McLUHAN   **181**

THE CITY   MARSHALL McLUHAN   **191**

YOU CAN SEE WHY THE MIGHTY WOULD BE CURIOUS
HOWARD GOSSAGE   **193**

**SUPPOSE HE IS WHAT HE SOUNDS LIKE, THE MOST IMPORTANT
THINKER SINCE NEWTON, DARWIN, FREUD, EINSTEIN, AND PAVLOV—
WHAT IF HE IS RIGHT?**   TOM WOLFE   **199**

STUDENT'S GUIDE 205

FOR EACH SELECTION: QUESTIONS FOR DISCUSSION

TOPICS FOR COMPOSITION

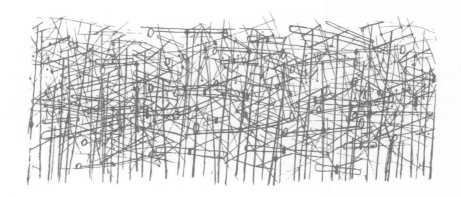

THE ROLE OF
THE MASS MEDIA

BEG → Into

The Mass Media

The media include television, radio, movies, newspapers, popular magazines, paperbacks, billboards, comic books. These are all deeply penetrated by advertising, by publicity campaigns and propaganda in open societies ~~like the United States~~, and by propaganda without commercial advertising in closed societies, like Russia. Hitler was an outstanding manipulator of propaganda. The bigger the lie, he said, the more massive the popular effect. And so it was under Hitler.

A good definition of the mass media is the delivery of a message to everybody, to the mass. The telephone delivers a message to a person, not to the mass. The Post Office delivers mail to specific individuals or organizations. Some magazines go to professional or specialized groups. The big "women's" magazines, however, are well within the category of mass media.

The danger in the mass media comes when some sender has an ulterior motive—to sell a product or sell a candidate or a policy. The fallacy of guilt by association, a form of propaganda directed against certain individuals, can be perpetrated from mouth to mouth, of course, but what really causes it to go to town are the mass media. Without the press and broadcasting, its effects would be limited. ~~How far would Senator Joe McCarthy have gone without his morning headline story on page one?~~

Before modern technology, the size of a community was strictly limited by the area over which messages could be sent. Without messages back and forth, government is impossible. The ancient empires of China, Persia, Rome, Peru were held together by roads over which swift runners or horsemen could carry orders.

Now a satellite in orbit can, in a split second, shower the whole planet with messages. "It is possible to maintain," Norbert Wiener once said, "that modern communication has made the World State inevitable." It was Dr. Wiener of M.I.T. who gave "cybernetics" to the world. The poet Archibald MacLeish emphasized the point when he observed that technology has produced the electronics for world-wide communication at the time when world-wide understanding must be achieved if we are to keep out of World War III.

Meanwhile, it is now possible to amplify a spoken word as much as a billion times, and replicate a written word indefinitely. ~~The question remains, however, whether a billion-fold amplification improves the message. Let us sample some highly amplified messages that came to the eyes and ears of untold Americans last Christmas.~~

2

END

Merry Christmas

Art Buchwald, with his ear to the commercials, forwards these Holiday Wishes:

*May you never have iron-poor blood or an
Excedrin headache. May your breath be always
fresh, and may you never perspire in case
someone in the family has made away with
the deodorant. God grant that you have the
wisdom to choose the right tooth paste. I pray
that your soap will give you twenty-four-hour
protection, and that you never develop
dishpan hands.*

*May you get more shaves with your blade
than with any other brand. May your
cigarettes always be mild, and their tar
content low. May your beer always be cold.
May the wax stay on your floors, and the
stains on your linen disappear in seconds.
May your peanut butter never stick to the
roof of your mouth.*

*May your bank be ever ready with a loan to
tide you over the rough places in life, and
may you never get stuck in the mud because
you used the wrong gasoline. May your spark
plugs spark, and your battery never run
down. And may you win thousands of dollars
at gas station sweepstakes.*

*Finally, I wish each and every one of you
instant tuning, a clear, ghost-free picture,
and on this holiday may all your TV tubes be bright.*

This is good fun, and better than a Ph.D. thesis for illuminating our affluent society.

STUART CHASE

THE MASS MEDIA AS "LANGUAGES"

ROY A. GALLANT

When you look through rose-tinted glasses, you see a rose-colored world, but your experience tells you that the world is not really rose-colored. But perhaps it is—to some creature whose eyes happen to admit only rosy light. To say that the world out there is *really* like this or that is impossible. We perceive it through what has passed the filters of our eyes, ears, fingers, and special sensing devices that we can build in the laboratory. But what is kept out by those filters cannot be known to us directly; and what is distorted by them can be only imperfectly known.

Languages are also filters, causing us to feel certain ways about the world, and causing us to react to the world in certain ways. Unfortunately, few of us can change "language filters" and feel the world as a speaker of Aivilik, Hopi, or Japanese feels it. As the language scholar S. I. Hayakawa said, the world out there, the *objective world,* is an intensely personal relationship between you and it.

The mass media of communications—TV, radio, newspapers, magazines, books, and motion pictures—are also filters which affect the way we see the world. They operate as languages by helping shape the world for us, each in its own way. You have seen many people cry over a movie or over a TV play, but hardly ever over a newspaper story. As we take our language for granted, we also take our mass media for granted. Yet, whenever we switch from one mass medium to another, we switch "language-filters." Each switch changes our perspective of the world in important ways. Radio, TV, a newspaper, a newsmagazine can all report the same event to us, but each plays on our emotions differently because it filters the message differently. These different filters play an invisible role in making us feel the way we do about a message.

Every student of journalism is taught that a news story must be written in a certain way. I am not talking about Sunday supplement "feature" stories or editorials. I am talking about the news stories that make up most of a newspaper. The first sentence of a news story is called the "lead." Its purpose is to give the reader the "most important" part of the story:

A Well Spurting Raw Oil into the Pacific Was Sealed Off Today with a Big Plug of Cement

The second paragraph has less important information and begins to fill in details about the lead.

Later paragraphs contain still less important information. This way of framing a news story is called the "inverted pyramid."

News stories are packaged in these standard molds for a very good reason.

A daily newspaper has to be written and printed in a rush. Each of the dozens of stories has to be positioned and tailored to fit a certain space on the page. Also, if a big story breaks at the last minute, the stories on the front page may have to be reshuffled. This may mean that one or more stories have to be shortened in a matter of a few minutes. Because the editor must work quickly and because there is usually not time to rewrite the story so that it will fit the new space, the editor cuts the story from the bottom up. He chops off the last and least important paragraph first, then the next to last paragraph, and so on up the pyramid until he has cut enough lines. The swift pace of daily newspaper publishing made the inverted pyramid story frame necessary, and newspapers still live with it. The motto of *The New York Times* is "All the News That's Fit To Print." Journalism students jokingly twist the thought around: "All the News That Fits, We Print."

Weekly newsmagazines frame their stories differently. A newsmagazine sells views about the news, not the news itself. The events it reports happened several days ago, or a week ago, so they are old hat from a newspaper point of view. The newsmagazine gives us news-in-depth by embroidering a story with background information and opinion. Also, the newsmagazine writer often tries to let a story unfold in a natural way. He tends to write his story by presenting events in the order in which they happened.

Free of the newspaper man's inverted pyramid, the newsmagazine writer can build drama into his story. Although the "lead" may be buried way down in the second, third, or a later paragraph, it often is the high point of a drama that has been holding the newsmagazine reader in suspense. When the reader finishes the story he has the impression that he now knows what *really* happened. But does he? Or does the frame within which the newsmagazine story has been cast make the reader feel the way he does because an "invisible filter" has been used?

Some time ago British thieves hijacked a shipment of gold in London. *The New York Times* reported the story in the traditional inverted pyramid frame. *Time* magazine framed the story in its own style. Here are both versions:

London Gang Takes $2-Million in Gold From a Bank Truck

Special to The New York Times

LONDON, May 1—Bandits hijacked a bank truck carrying bullion today and escaped with about $2-million worth of gold bars.

The raid took place shortly before noon in the Islington section of Northeast London as the driver and two guards in the van were finishing their second delivery.

The gang, said to number from six to 10, apparently used ammonia and clubs to subdue the driver and guards.

The theft involved about 144 gold bars weighing 1.9 tons and was the largest of its kind in Britain.

The record bullion theft was the still unsolved robbery of German national gold reserves by a group of United States soldiers and German civilians in Bavaria in June, 1945, shortly after the defeat of Nazi Germany. In that theft, a total of 730 gold bars valued at almost $10-million, along with six bags of bank notes and 25 boxes of platinum bars and precious stones, were taken.

Nor did today's haul equal that of the "Great Train Robbery" in Britain in 1963, when a gang robbed a mail train of British currency worth $7,268,000.

The bullion that figured in today's robbery had been loaded aboard the truck of N. M. Rothschild & Sons, the bankers, at its refinery near the Tower of London.

The bars were loose in the back of the truck as it set off to make four deliveries.

While the truck was unloading some silver solution at Breloques, Ltd., a concern of jewelers in Bowling Green Lane, the gang struck.

Then, the police said, the gang, or at least some members of it, drove the van off at high speed in a northwesterly direction.

After about 20 minutes of driving the van stopped suddenly, and the 144 gold bars were removed from the rear compartment, apparently into another vehicle.

Once again, according to the van crew's account to the police, the van drove on again for a short distance and then stopped. It was found abandoned by the thieves about two miles away from the scene of the raid.

The guards and driver, blindfolded and bound with adhesive tape, were left in the van's rear compartment. They managed to attract the attention of four women, who were on their way to a bingo parlor, by banging on the truck's sides and calling for help. The entire operation lasted 35 minutes.

While one of the guards was delivering the silver solution, the driver and the other guard moved the truck up the street a bit because of vehicles parked in front of the jewelry concern.

As the guard was returning to the van he was seized from behind by one or more members of the gang. At the same moment the driver and the other guard in the van heard a tapping on the vehicle's rear door.

Assuming it was the returning guard, they opened the door, when, according to the police, ammonia was sprayed into their faces and they were hit with clubs. The victims told the police that the gang members did not say a word during the raid.

The police and customs officials at seaports and airports were alerted and the markings on the gold bars were circulated among precious metal dealers.

However, the police conceded that, although it would be a difficult operation with such a cumbersome haul, the gold could find its way into some hidden smelter, be melted down and then sold in small quantities to dealers.

The driver and the guards were taken to hospitals with head, chest and eye injuries.

GREAT BRITAIN

As Good as Gold

The week's wash hung out to dry in the fitful Monday sunshine, the good ladies of Kentish Town, London, stepped out for their afternoon bingo game. As one bunch of Mums passed a blue truck parked in a side street, a voice cried out: "Lady, lady, will you phone the police? We are tied up in here." "Ah, you're having us on," replied Maude Smyth, 50, the archetype of English womanhood, from home perm to sensible walking shoes. "Truly, lady," came the very English reply from inside, "if you look through the crack you'll see us trussed up like chickens." Maude Smyth and her three stout companions looked, and great consternation followed. For the bingo ladies of Kentish Town were the first to learn about Britain's crime of the year: the theft of $2,100,000 worth of gold bullion.

What Twiggy is doing for fashions, a new breed of audacious British thieves is doing for crime. British crime has become both more frequent and more spectacular ever since the Great Train Robbery of 1963 whetted rascals' appetites for neatly executed commando-type operations—and titillated the imagination of millions with tales of rags to riches. British robbers these days are getting away with an incredible $840,000 in loot each week.

Silent Thieves. The truck that Maude Smyth spotted belonged to N. M. Rothschild & Sons, a firm of merchant bankers. It was making routine deliveries of gold bullion to dealers about London when it stopped, as usual, to drop a bag of silver worth $14 at a small printing shop on Bowling Green Lane. As the guard who delivered the silver bag was walking back to his truck, he was hit from behind. Hearing the usual two-knock signal, his companions opened the roll-up door in the back. Instantly, their eyes were blinded by a liquid squirted from a gas gun. "It was so fast we didn't have a chance. We couldn't even get to our coshes [billy clubs]," said one guard. Blindfolded, hands and feet bound with adhesive tape, the three Rothschild men were driven to an unknown rendezvous, where the silent thieves—believed to have numbered ten in all—relieved the truck of its contents: 144 gold bars weighing 1.7 tons.

The loot, unsalable in Britain, must be got out. But how? In Alec Guinness' *Lavender Hill Mob*, the gold was melted down into souvenir miniatures of the Eiffel Tower and shipped to Paris. In Ian Fleming's *Goldfinger*, the villain fled England in a Rolls-Royce whose body was made of solid gold. Scotland Yard has boarded and inspected all ships departing England—so far to no avail. Somewhere in England, the 144 gold bricks, whose telltale markings can easily be erased by melting, were probably bubbling merrily in a cauldron.

When the late James Thurber was a newspaper reporter his editor told him to write short, dramatic leads to stories. The shorter the better. Thurber reportedly wrote the following lead for a murder story: Dead. That's what the man was when they found him with a knife in his back at 4 P.M. in front of Riley's saloon at the corner of 52nd and 12th Streets.

In the newspaper inverted pyramid account of the theft, the first 18 words of the story tell you what happened. Thereafter, if need be, the story could be chopped at the end of any paragraph. You would never feel the difference. In the news magazine account, it is not until after the 125th word that you find out what the story is about, but then you already know because you read last week's newspaper. The only paragraph the magazine account could do without is the second. The last paragraph might not seem necessary, but it contains important information, that of disposing of the gold. Also, the last paragraph, like the first, is a point-of-view maker. Both are mood-setters that cunningly prepare you to enter and exit from the story as if it were a fun house.

Two people, one of whom had read only the newspaper account and the other of whom had read only the magazine account, meet and discuss the theft. One is amused by it, the other is not. The fact is that both are reacting as much to the way the story was framed (the medium) as they are to the story itself (the content). Each saw it through a different filter.

When radio and TV report an event they frame the message in still different ways. They involve us by touching our emotions in ways that the printed word cannot. Listening to radio is like sitting in the dark and talking. The words seem close, rich, more intense, and take on shades of meaning that they lack on the printed page. The tone of voice a skillful announcer uses can sooth, anger, excite, or persuade us.

To hear the poets Dylan Thomas or E. E. Cummings read their works is to be drawn into their world with an intensity that the printed page cannot give us. The poet Archibald MacLeish wrote: "The technique of radio has developed tools which could not have been more perfectly adapted to the poet's uses had he devised them himself."

Person-to-person speech is radio's major strength. An interview on radio involves us much more than a printed version of the interview does. In a newspaper or magazine interview we do not hear the silky voice, or the gravelly, faltering voice that we hear on a radio interview. We react not only to the words spoken but to the quality of the voice. In some cases the quality of the voice may sway our opinion, not what the voice is saying. In print we have to be told that the voice is gravelly and faltering. Add a picture to the voice, as TV does, and we can see the anxious face belonging to the voice. The voice, the shape of the face, the cut of the dress or suit—each in its own way colors our response to what the person is saying. Perhaps they shouldn't, we say, but surely they do. And try as we may to be objective, we cannot be.

The movies are still another window on the world, framing our impressions of what is "out there" in yet another way. The early film makers nearly always set up their cameras at two fixed distances from the actors—the long shot or the medium shot. It was an attempt to give the audience the "natural" view of the stage, the view people were accustomed to in a theater. Then in 1908 the imaginative director D. W. Griffith hit on the idea of the close-up. Viewers of the film *After Many Years* were astonished by a giant close-up suddenly appearing in the middle of a scene. Hollywood had begun to discover what a powerful medium film could be.

"The close-up," according to Erik Barnouw of Columbia University, "began to give audiences a new kind of intimacy with the heroes and heroines of the story. Soon films were full of close-ups. Soon millions of men knew, more exactly than the features of their own wives, the tilt of a movie heroine's nose and the arch of her eyebrow. It is no accident that the star system began a year or two after Griffith's use of close-ups."

In more recent years the giant screen has added another bigger-than-life dimension to the movies. In *Lawrence of Arabia* the magnificent sweeping scenes of the desert reduced the actors to props. The desert commanded our attention, our feelings, not the action that took place on it.

Close-up and panoramic scenes, which the movies handle so well, were doomed on TV. On the motion picture screen each individual eyelash and tear of the weeping heroine stands out in sharp relief. On a TV screen such details are lost and the face in a close-up becomes a blur. The panoramic scene on TV fails for the same reason. Details are lost. An aerial view of the Grand Canyon becomes a blur. The electronic coarseness of the TV screen has forced the TV camera to settle for the medium-distance shot. Old movies are much better in the movie house than they are on TV. When Hollywood discovered why and began making movies tailored for TV, it stayed away from the giant close-up and other camera shots that depend on fine detail for impact.

BACK TO LANGUAGE

Like languages, the mass media frame our impressions of the world in a variety of ways. But the mass media are not languages, any more than the dance of honeybees or the courtship displays of the green heron are languages. Language is a distinctively human activity.

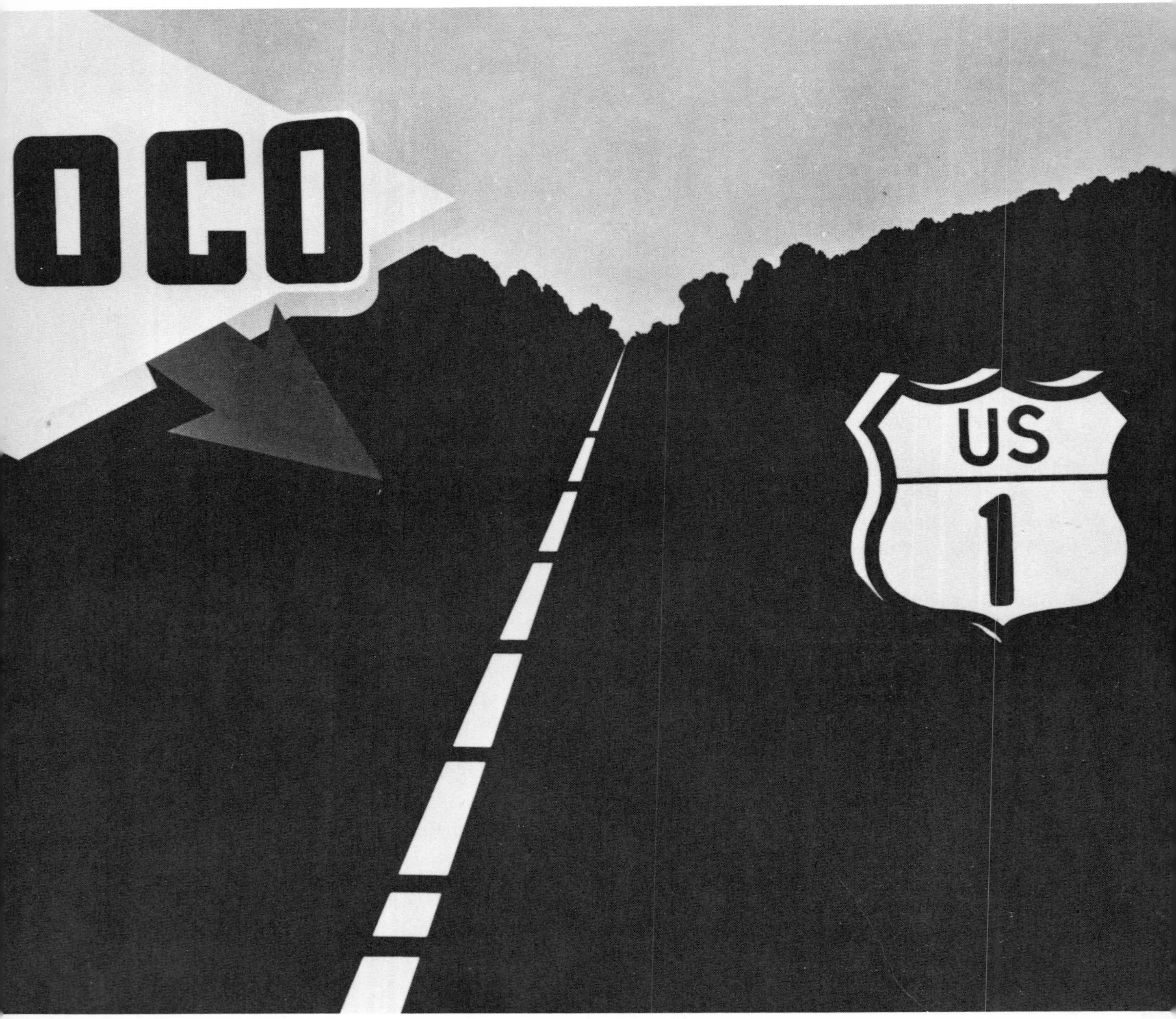
OCO
US
1

THE MASS MEDIA—A BALANCE SHEET   STUART CHASE

n my book *The Power of Words,* I tried to draw a balance sheet for the mass media, and concluded that on the whole the liabilities exceeded the assets. Now, a dozen years later, I see no reason to revise this overall estimate. But the triumph of television in showing three brave men orbiting the moon in December 1968 went a long way toward building up the assets. This chapter and this book will end with one man's reaction to that extraordinary performance.

BALANCE SHEET

LIABILITIES OF THE MASS MEDIA

1. The media can be used as a weapon by dictators. The first move in a military coup is to seize the local broadcasting station. Hitler, Mussolini, Stalin, Franco, Péron—could they have held supreme power without tight control of radio and press? Now TV gives a dictator an even firmer grip. But we must remember that the converse also occurs. The TV broadcasts of Senator Joe McCarthy's hearings disgusted many viewers with his furious, ranting style and intemperate accusations. TV played a large part, first in his rise to notoriety, and later in his downfall.

2. The mass media amplify campaign oratory in the democracies, much of it meaningless. "Let us rekindle the sacred fire of liberty" . . . "I view with alarm and incredulity the misdeeds of the opposition" . . . "No sacrifice is too great" . . . "We must not flag in our historic mission" . . . "We will leave no stone unturned" . . . "You never had it so good" . . . "Turn the rascals out." James Reston, reporting the Republican convention in 1968, pointed out: "Republicans are proclaiming domestic and foreign goals which they are not prepared to pay for, and even the delegates in Miami Beach somehow know that there is a gap between the campaign rhetoric and the reality of the country and world at large."

3. Hollywood movies have broadcast a distorted image of the United States abroad. By exporting the "bang! bang! you're dead!" masterpieces of the silver screen, we lead our neighbors to believe that six-shooters are actually more common than wristwatches along Fifth Avenue.

4. Entertainment takes a long march ahead of education. When real information is given, it is often carefully packaged, like powdered coffee.

5. Conflict hits the front page; agreement the back page. The news from Vietnam was spiced with a "body count," which nobody believed.

6. The mass media can make a Galahad out of a nobody. "Shine, mister?" "Build you up, mister?" A whole profession of public relations is based on this dubious process. Most people want a leader, somebody to believe in and follow. The media can circulate an *image* of Congressman Blowhard which is a long way from reality. The image gets the votes; the voters later get the trouble.

7. The mass media, as used by advertisers, have done much to increase air and water pollution, by wasteful consumption. Now they are amplifying noise pollution.

8. Billboards continue to multiply along highways and railways, making a comely landscape hideous, not to mention an increase in traffic accidents.

9. The mass media spread the news of violence instantly and thus encourage imitation. An airplane hijacked today becomes three tomorrow. One student demonstration—and presto!—cops on a dozen campuses.

10. Finally, there is the effect of TV on children. Watching it more hours a day tends to alienate them from parents and natural environment.

There are other serious liabilities to be levied against the mass media, but the above are perhaps the major ones.

ASSETS OF THE MASS MEDIA

1. The mass media now widely disseminate the news of the world. Where is a tribe in the jungle without its village radio?

2. They have provided good music—and some not so good—to an enormous audience.

3. They are helping children get a better education in school.

4. They can warn us of coming heat waves, frosts, blizzards, floods, hurricanes. Presently they may do something about cyclones and earthquakes.

5. They can save lives, for instance, by telling ocean shipping, helicopters and Coast Guard vessels where to reach a ship in distress, pick up the survivors and render first aid.

6. They have made life supportable to many invalids, and to the blind and deaf.

7. The mass media are paving the way for One World, as Norbert Wiener observed, where every person alive can be reached through the communication networks almost instantly.

ON BALANCE

Where does the balance lie? I repeat that the net effect to my mind is negative. Scanning the advertisements in the Sunday edition of our newspapers convinces me that sponsor and agent are primarily devoted to exploiting human weakness. Here are emphatic, if not brazen, appeals to snobbery, vanity, greed, fear. It is apparently illegal to run an ad for travel abroad without a girl in a bikini inviting you with outstretched arms.

Man is the animal with the big brain, seldom employed at capacity. He is capable of using it to improve his condition, and the time is running short. The mass media, however, deliberately or not, tend to downgrade his native intelligence. If a consumer, let us say, has an I.Q. of 120, he is pushed back to 95 by this vigorous attack on his prejudices, appetites and weaknesses. The shrewdest brains in our country are hard at work devising ploys against the reasoning ability of citizens. This is not only bad for the citizen, but bad for the community—however stimulating it may be to the Gross National Product.

The implicit fact about TV is that you have no *interaction* with it. A child sitting in front of a set gets no personal experience in influencing other people, or being influenced by them. Is there a connection between this four-hour-a-day exposure, and the large number of youngsters from educated and middle-class families who find it hard, if not impossible, to relate to any belief system in the culture—and who therefore drop out?

MOONSHOT

After this gloomy prognosis, we turn to a more cheerful aspect of television, and a very large asset indeed.

I am sitting in a comfortable chair in my living room at Christmas time in 1968, and see the forbidding landscape of the moon, 70 miles away, as it looks to an astronaut. I can hear him describe how it looks: "Yes, we are right over the crater of Copernicus."

This is not a Hollywood act, not even a tape, but a live message from Colonel Frank Borman, commander of the Apollo 8 spacecraft, speaking to eager watchers, some 200 million of them, on Planet Earth. Presently he shifts his TV camera and shows us our little bobbing planet as it looks to him, partly lighted by the sun, with the South Pole up at the right-hand corner, beyond a dim outline of South America.

"Is it inhabited?" he asks, half smiling.

Yes, Colonel, it is inhabited, at least for the moment. But we cannot promise how long it will be inhabited. There is enough nuclear overkill in stock in the U.S. and the U.S.S.R. to wipe out most forms of life.

The mass media present serious liabilities, but with this message from Colonel Borman coming into our living rooms, they are putting the territory, the world outside our heads, into magnificent and unprecedented perspective. We are seeing events and hearing words unique in human experience. That little, half-illumined sphere down there, 238,857 miles away, is our only home. All humanity, save for three bold astronauts, is there below those clouds. Below those clouds the air, water, trees, grass, and throbbing life.

Can our children, or our children's children—whatever the synthetic environment which science may provide—can they endure the utter bleakness and loneliness of the pock-marked desolation we see from the spacecraft's window, seventy miles away? Can they endure the desolation of Venus, or of Mars? Can they go to live on a planet circling the nearest star, said to be four light-years away? Not until the physicists can find a force faster than the speed of light to carry our children there; faster than 186,000 miles per second. Colonel Borman's maximum was 24,000 miles per hour, less than seven miles per second.

The editors and the commentators are on their feet talking, nay shouting, of the great release: "Mankind assaults the universe! We reach our hands out to the stars!" Easy, gentlemen, easy. But certainly electronics has widened our horizons, quite literally. Will this view from the rim of the moon help us do what must be done there on the turning earth?

I darken the screen and sit here wondering.

TELEVISION

Every minute of television programming—commercials, entertainment, news—
teaches us something.
NICHOLAS JOHNSON

It turns out that TV is a powerful educational medium even when it isn't trying
to be, even when it's only trying to entertain. There must be millions of people
who have learned, simply by watching crime dramas in the past few years, that
they have the right to remain silent when arrested.
HERB SCHLOSSER

The presentation of news and ideas is never, in practice, totally separated from
entertainment values.
GILBERT SELDES

It was the funeral of President Kennedy that most strongly proved the power
of television to invest an occasion with the character of corporate participation.
It involves an entire population in a ritual process. By comparison, press,
movies, and radio are mere packaging devices for consumers.
MARSHALL McLUHAN

Until a few years ago every American assumed he possessed an equal and
God-given expertise on three things: politics, religion, and the weather. Now a
fourth has been added—television.
ERIC SEVAREID

I can preach to more people in one night on TV than perhaps Paul did in his
whole lifetime.
BILLY GRAHAM

not

A great deal of what has been done has been excellent by any standards, and it has vastly increased people's understanding of human nature, literature, and even history. Through television we realize that we are all one, all over the world.
KENNETH CLARK

Television is a medium of expression which permits millions of people to listen to the same joke at the same time, and yet remain lonesome.
T. S. ELIOT

Popular commercial TV is not likely to face life's facts when it wants to leave a viewer in a serene state of mind.
JACK GOULD, *The New York Times*

We are human and, given a chance, we still might create an art form of television.
GILBERT SELDES

The video cassette revolution is hardly an adequate description for a technological upheaval that will likely do to television what television did to radio.
GENE YOUNGBLOOD

A Nation of Videots

An Interview
with Jerzy Kosinski

by DAVID SOHN

Interviewer (Sohn): Edmund Carpenter, the noted anthropologist, observed that every medium has it own grammar—the elements which enable it to communicate. McLuhan also—with his "the medium is the message"—talked about how a medium communicates.

KOSINSKI: I tend to think in terms of a medium's recipients, not in terms of the medium itself. A television set without viewers doesn't interest me. Television as a technical process doesn't interest me either. Yet the role television plays in our lives does interest me very much.

Interviewer: Isn't that related to what you were saying in your book, *Being There?*

KOSINSKI: The main character of *Being There,* Chance, has no meaningful existence outside of what he experiences on television. Unlike the reader of fiction who re-creates a text arbitrarily in his imagination, Chance, who cannot read or fantasize, is at the mercy of the tube. He cannot imagine himself functioning in anything but the particular situations offered him by TV programs. Of course, Chance is a fictional archetype. On the other hand, a number of teachers have told me that many of their young students resemble Chance. A child begins school nowadays with basic images from "his own garden"—television.

Children have always imitated adults, but "TV babies," with access to a world beyond that of their parents and siblings, often mimic TV personalities. They behave according to TV models, not according to their moods, and their actions reflect patterns they have picked up from television. They're funny à la Don Rickles or Chico and Sanford; they're tough like Kojak or Khan.

The basic difference, for me, between television and the novel as media is that television takes the initiative: it does the involving. It says, "You, the passive spectator, are there. Stay there. I'll do the moving, talking, acting." Frenetic, quick-paced, engineered by experts in visual drama, everything from a thirty-second commercial to a two-hour movie is designed to fit into neat time slots, wrapped up in lively colors and made easily digestible.

While viewing, you can eat, you can recline, you can walk around the set, you can even change channels, but you won't lose contact with the medium. Unlike theater or cinema, TV allows, even encourages, all these "human" diversions. TV's hold on you is so strong, it is not easily threatened or severed by "the other life" you lead (While watching, you are not reminded (as you would be by a theater audience, for instance) that you are a member of society whose thoughts and reactions may be valuable. You are isolated and given no time to reflect. The images rush on and you cannot stop them or slow them down or turn them back.)

Recently I heard of a college class in media communication which had been assigned to watch two hours of television and record the content of those two hours. They were asked to describe each element—including commercials—in as much detail as possible, classifying every incident and every character in terms of its relative importance to the story. All these students had been raised in front of TV sets and were accustomed to being bombarded by TV images; many of them hoped to be employed in the communications industry after graduation. Yet, not a single one could complete the assignment. They claimed that the rapidity and fragmentation of the TV experience made it impossible to isolate a narrative thought-line, or to contemplate and analyze what they had seen, in terms of relative significance.

Interviewer: Have you ever noticed, when you go to someone's house, that very often the television set will be on and it continues on? In fact, people leave it on all day.

KOSINSKI: Many of us do. I watch it a lot. In my apartment, for instance, my visiting friends often get very jittery around 7 p.m. They want to see the news. I turn the television on and, for an hour, we all cruise around it. We're still talking to each other, or drinking with each other, but we have been disconnected—we are now *being there,* in that other world "brought to you by . . ."—the medium's crucial phrase.

Yet the viewer knows that he is not Columbo or Captain Kangaroo. He is separated from the stars not only by his patently different identity, being *here* while they are *there,* but also—and this is far more important—by the very process of watching, of having been assigned the role of spectator. In this process, the spectator occupies one world, while what he views comes from another. The bridge between the two is TV's absolutely concrete nature. Every situation it portrays is particular: every descriptive detail is given, nothing is implied, no blank spaces are left for the viewer to fill in.

Now, literature is general, made up of words which are often vague, or which represent many classes of things: for instance, "tree," "bird," "human being." A novel becomes concrete only through the reader's own imagining or staging-from-within, which is grounded in his memory, his fancy, his current reality. . . . The printed page offers nothing but "inking"; the reader provides his own mental props, his own emotional and physical details. From the infinite catalog of his mind, the reader picks out the things which were most interesting to him, most vivid, most memorable as defined by his own life.

Because it is uncontrolled and totally free, this process offers unexpected, unchannelled·associations, new insights into the tides and drifts of one's own life. The reader is tempted to venture beyond a text, to contemplate his own life in light of the book's personalized meanings.(Television, though, doesn't demand any such inner reconstruction. Everything is already there, explicit, ready to be watched, to be followed on its own terms, at the speed it dictates. The viewer is given no time to pause, to recall, to integrate the image-attack into his own experience.)

Interviewer: I'm intrigued by your analysis of how television influences our self-perception and behavior.

KOSINSKI: During the years when I was teaching, I invited several seven- to ten-year-old children into a very large classroom where two video monitors were installed, one on the left side and one on the right side of the blackboard. TV cameras were also placed on either side of the room. I sat before the blackboard, telling a story. Suddenly, an intruder from outside rushed into the room—prearranged, of course—and started arguing with me, pushing and hitting me. The cameras began filming the incident, and the fracas appeared on both screens of the monitors, clearly visible to all the children. Where did the kids look? At the event (the attacker and me), or at the screen? According to the video record of a third camera, which filmed the students' reactions, the majority seldom.looked at the actual incident in the center of the room. Instead, they turned toward the screens which were placed above eye-level and therefore easier to see than the real event. Later, when we talked about it, many of the children explained that they could see the attack better on the screens. After all, they pointed out, they could see close-ups of the attacker and of me, his hand on my face, his expressions—all the details they wanted— without being frightened by "the real thing" (or by the necessity of becoming involved).

At another time, I showed short educational 16mm films on the video, while telling the children—again from seven to ten years old—that something fascinating was happening in the corridor. "Now those who want to stay inside and watch the films are free to remain in the class," I said, "but there's something really incredible going on outside, and those who want to see it are free to leave the room." No more than ten percent of the children left. I repeated, "You know *what's outside is really fantastic. You have never seen it before.* Why don't you just step out and take a look?" And they always said, "No, no, no, we prefer to stay here and watch the film." I'd say, "But you don't know what's outside." "Well, what is it?" they'd ask. "You have to go find out." And they'd say, "Why don't we just sit here and see the film first?" There it was: they were already too lazy, too corrupted to get up and take a chance on "the outside."

Interviewer: That's an incredible indictment of television.

KOSINSKI: Not of television as much as of a society founded on the principle of passive entertainment. When I was attacked by the intruder, for instance, the kids were less interested in the actual assault than in what the TV cameras were doing—as if they had paid to see a film, as if the incident had been staged to entertain them! And all during the confrontation—despite my yelling, his threats, the fear that I showed—the kids did not interfere or offer to help. None of them.

They sat transfixed as if the TV cameras neutralized the act of violence. And perhaps they did. By filming a brutal physical struggle from a variety of viewpoints, the cameras transformed a human conflict into an aesthetic happening, distancing the audience and allowing them an alternative to moral judgment and involvement . . .

Later on I interviewed them about what had happened in the class. Most of them said, "Well, you know, these cameras were set up, and then, you know, this guy came and pushed you, and well, it was kind of, uh, you could see him and you on these screens very well. You looked so scared and he was so mean." I asked, "What do you mean, you could see it very well?" "Well, you know, you could see *everything* on those screens. They are great. How much does it cost to buy one of these videos?"

Interviewer: That's eerie. What does it all mean?

KOSINSKI: I can only guess. It's obviously related to the fact that so many kids prefer to stay home and watch TV than to go to a museum, explore the city, or even play with their peers. They can see close-ups, and commercials, and when bored, shift to another channel. We've reached the point now where people—adults and children alike—would prefer to watch a televised ballgame than to sit in some far corner of a stadium, too hot or too cold, uncomfortable, surrounded by a smelly crowd, with no close-ups, no other channel to turn to. Uncomfortable—like life often is.

Interviewer: In regard to television and education, are there any beneficial effects that you can put your finger on?

KOSINSKI: For me, the word "beneficial" doesn't apply to television. TV is simply a part of contemporary life. I must confront it, think about it, accept it, or reject it.

Interviewer: It's part of the environment, and therefore difficult to perceive.

KOSINSKI: Yes, perhaps because it exists in a very uneasy relationship with the environment. The medium is so overwhelming. How do you assess the importance of an activity which accompanies you practically all the time? The average working American apparently watches it for 1,200 hours per year while, for instance, book-reading occupies only five hours of his time. How do you judge its role in our political life? The impact of its commercialism? Of its ordering of time? Of its ranking of what's important (therefore visible) and what's not (therefore left out)?

Interviewer: You can notice certain things. For example, children coming to school these days have been affected by "Sesame Street" and "The Electric Company" and some of the other programs. When they come to kindergarten they already know their letters and numbers. In the same vein, older people suddenly have better access to the world, a chance to see much more than ever before.

KOSINSKI: Let's say better access to the world *of television.* In small European communities still without television, the old people remain physically active, mixing with the young, venturing out into the real world. Here, like their little grandchildren, they sit immobilized by TV. An American senior citizen once told me that his TV set gave him a sixth sense—at the price of removing the other five. I think that both young and old are acquiring, via television, a superficial glimpse of a narrow slice of unreality. I'm not certain how such "knowledge" is used, or what it does. Does it make real life more meaningful or individuals more active? Does it encourage adventure? Does it arm an individual against the pains inflicted by society, by other humans, by aging? Does it bring us closer to each other? Does it explain us to ourselves, and ourselves to each other? Does it?

For me, imagining groups of solitary individuals watching their private, remote-controlled TV sets is the ultimate future terror: a nation of *videots.*

One thing I am convinced of is that human conduct is primarily determined by human intercourse—by the relationship of one being with another being. So anything which is detrimental to that interaction, anything which delays it, makes it more uneasy, or creates a state of apprehension, is detrimental to the growing of society.

I look at the children who spend five or six hours watching television every day, and I notice that when in groups they cannot interact with each other. They are terrified of each other; they develop secondary anxiety characteristics. They want to watch, they don't want to be spoken to. They want to watch, they don't want to talk. They want to watch, they don't want to be asked questions or singled out.

TV also influences the way they view the world. On television, the world is exciting, single-faceted, never complex. By comparison, their own lives appear slow, uneventful, bewildering. They find it easier to watch televised portrayals of human experiences—violence, love, adventure, sex—than to gain the experience for themselves. They believe in avoiding real contests just as they believe in pain killers and sleeping pills. It was TV that first taught them to rely on drugs, that there was no need to suffer, to be tense or unhappy or even uncomfortable, because a drug would relieve all that. Even death is no longer a necessary part of existence for them. Its finality is gone because their hero, no matter how dead, would rise again.

So they grow up essentially mute. As teenagers, they are anxious to join an amorphous group—a rock band or a film audience. The music or the film relieves them of all necessity to interact with each other—the blaring sounds prevent communication, the screen above their heads is the focus of all their attention. They remain basically mute: sitting *with* each other, *next* to each other, but *removed from* each other by this omnipresent third party—music or film.

Silence and the absence of entertainment are more than discomforts to TV generations—they are threats. They cause anxiety. I think silence is an invitation to reflection or to conversation, the prime terrors to videots. One of the TV talk show hosts once said to me that "this is the only country in the world where people watch conversation every night." . . .

For me silence and solitude are necessary for self redefinition, for daily reassessing the purpose of my life. Silence occurs when I consider *who* I am, when I read fiction or poetry. Reading and writing are part of my confronting myself and society. Of my own rages and resignations.

Interviewer: It would seem, then, that television may be robbing us of our fantasy life.

KOSINSKI: A TV show is a product of people, many of whom are first rank artists, profoundly creative, inventive, concerned with their work and with its impact on the public. But, by its very nature, a TV show is, above all, a result of a *collective* (not individual) fantasy. It is subjected to various collective influences, collective editing, collective simplifying, collective sponsorship, etc. In other words, *"Brought to you by . . ."*

But television has another characteristic as well, one that we tend to overlook. It's a portable multi-theater. If, while viewing, you're upset by one of the programs, you don't have to get up, leave it, and walk the street to reach another theater and pay to see another show. You just press a button, and you are transferred to another place. Thus, at any time, you can step out of one collective fantasy and step into another. That effortless control over an activity that occupies so much of our time is profoundly affecting. After all, such effortless freedom doesn't exist in any other domain of our life.

Let's assume that, right now, in the middle of our conversation, you angered me and I decided to leave in midsentence, without warning. First, in order to define my anger, I would have to reflect, to decide why I don't want to sit with you anymore or why I should leave. Then I would have to decide how I should go about leaving: Should I push the table away and reveal my anger, or, rather, should I make up some excuse? Should I tell you what I think of you and expose myself to potential abuse, or should I say nothing? It would be a conflict situation, complex, difficult to resolve and painful. Still, quite common to us all.

Yet, watching a similar conflict on television would in no way prepare me emotionally to confront and handle such a situation in reality. As a teacher, what can I learn from "McMillan and Wife"? As a foreign-born, can I really absorb the idiom of "McCloud"? As a novelist, can I benefit from the calmness and insight of "Columbo"? And as an officer of P.E.N. (the international association of writers), would I imitate the practices depicted in "The Name of the Game"?

What TV Is Doing To America

An Interview with Alistair Cooke

Reprinted from *U.S. News & World Report*

The Influence of Television

Interviewer: Mr. Cooke, what are the most striking effects on Americans of a quarter century of widespread television?

COOKE: The most striking thing to me is that television has produced a generation of children who have a declining grasp of the English language but also have a visual sophistication that was denied to their parents. They learn so much about the world that appeals immediately to their emotions, but I'm not sure it involves their intelligence, their judgment.

Interviewer: Are you suggesting that they have a great random knowledge but not an understanding of what it is they know?

COOKE: More or less. Things can come at you on television in a flash—in three seconds—which would take a fine teacher an hour or so to interpret. I noticed this every day of the two years that we were filming the "America" series.

Of course, I wrote as pithily as I could, as one must on television. Time and again I had to reduce an argument to two minutes, and then to a minute and 30 seconds, if I was in good form. Yet very often one sentence, and a picture and a chord of music, can give the essence of what you are trying to say. .

Interviewer: What effect is television having on American society and the generation formed by this new experience?

COOKE: It's awfully hard to tell. There's the problem that we are all getting more information now than we can cope with.

I think that's the reason for the sort of low-key hysteria—Thoreau's "quiet desperation"—that a lot of us live in. The images overwhelm our ability to make judgments or handle our government and our lives because we are so continuously aware of the disruption that's going on everywhere.

Television and Violence

Interviewer: Is our society more violent than it used to be because of television? Would the race riots and campus riots of the 1960s have happened without television being on hand to film the events?

COOKE: I think the race riots would have happened anyway. Telvision quick-ened the general awareness of the blacks' chronic plight. That's the good side of it.

But television can also spark trouble, especially among sick people. It can trigger fashions—whether in "streaking" or in kidnaping. And I think sick or defeated—really insane—people have been given, through television, the imagination to plan or contemplate violent acts.

The most terrifying thing to me is the instant publicity that television can give to bad news, which can then be copied anywhere in the world. There's no way out of that. There is a behavioral scientist in Dallas who says the only way to cure the kidnaping plague is to deny kidnapers the media, both newspapers and television.

Interviewer: How can television be regulated to minimize this extremely disruptive, almost revolutionary impact on a society?

COOKE: Since the main commitment of television and any other news media is to get out the news, I don't see how they can fairly edit out terror. . . .

Interviewer: How do the networks know that there is a public demand for such things as violence?

COOKE: They just look at the rating system, which they accept as statistical gospel. But an awful lot of people use television as sort of audible wallpaper. That is, they argue, quarrel, sleep, play cards against it. The ratings say, "This is what people are looking at." But it's what they *would be looking at* if they cared to.

Interviewer: Who really runs television?

COOKE: Well, the people who bear the responsibility for the programs are the network presidents and the advertising agencies.

Interviewer: Do the television producers simply respond to a marketable demand for violent or superficial programs?

COOKE: There's no question that they respond to what will sell a product. We often forget that in our country the primary function of television is that of a merchant. But people forget that if gun play and neurotic families sell more detergents than classical drama and documentaries on saving our landscape, they'll get gun play and serials.

Public and Commercial Television

Interviewer: Is public television the alternative?

COOKE: In our society I think you have to have both public and private television. All the media should provide a service for the widest possible variety of people.

Interviewer: Does that mean the lowest common denominator?

COOKE: No. It should mean the *highest* common denominator. That's what television should aim at.

Interviewer: Would it be desirable or necessary in the U.S. eventually to follow somewhat the British pattern, where there is much tighter control over programming and commercials?

COOKE: It depends upon who has the control. A misunderstanding that's very current in the United States is that the alternative to television run by networks for sponsors is to have "government-owned" television.

Well, British television is not government-owned in any sense that the Spanish or the French is. It's a public corporation, maintained by the public's paying a license fee for owning a set. It's bound by the acts of Parliament, but it's never bound by the policies of the Government. In fact, most governments dread the BBC's independence to do as it pleases.

Some years ago, there was protest about the BBC monopoly, and eventually Parliament allowed another network. But the interesting thing to point out is the way the British run their commercial network. On that network, it is not the advertisers—as in America—who bring you Alec Guinness or Julie Andrews. They buy time the way an advertiser for a newspaper buys space. They don't see a dry run of your editorial as a pilot before they buy. Advertisers on commercial television in Great Britain have no idea what they're buying, except that obviously a minute at noon costs less than a minute in prime time.

In other words, the advertiser is kept away from *production.* That's the important thing. The production companies put their shows on the commercial network and are just as free as the production teams employed by the BBC to do their own thing to the best of their ability. They are freed from outside, self-serving pressures.

Interviewer: Does this mean that the advertiser—the man who buys time—has no voice whatsoever in the content of the show where his product is advertised?

COOKE: That's right, because he doesn't *sponsor* a given program. He picks a certain time and pays according to whether it's prime time or not.

It's interesting that the Royal Commission that came over here to study commercial television made a big point in its recommendations about the program that I happened to be concerned with, in the early days of American television, which was called "Omnibus."

The Ford Foundation originally gave a grant to underwrite the show so that it would break even in case it didn't get sponsors. In fact, it got sponsors right away, but they had no idea what was coming up on the show. They simply bought a slot of time. They didn't know if they were going to have a Greek tragedy or the birth of a bee, an opera or a program on the central nervous system. On the production side, we did what we wanted to do, and it was too bad if the sponsors didn't like it.

Interviewer: Should we adopt the British system and finance our television with a license?

COOKE: I don't think it would be politically possible. There is, after all, federal funding for the public broadcasting system, and people who want to pay $15 a year can provide the balance that the system needs. It seems to me that having started with a completely commercial system, we probably never will be able to swing over. . . .

Interviewer: Was "Omnibus" a commercial success?

COOKE: Very much so till the last three or four years. In fact, it was the Canadians—Aluminium Ltd.—who kept us going.

The network theory was that "Omnibus" was a "minority" show. The producer pointed out to the network people that we then had 13.25 million families watching "Omnibus"—bigger than the total readership of *Time, Life, Look, The Reader's Digest* and *The Saturday Evening Post.* But it couldn't match Ed Sullivan and Jackie Gleason. . . .

Politics, War, and TV News

Interviewer: Basically, what is television's impact on politics?

COOKE: Oh, it's enormous. First of all, it has drastically simplified the convention game. Television has exposed the whole mechanism of politics. In the old days, we preserved our ideals and read only what we wanted to read. But today many, many more people know how cities are run, how conventions are run, how bills go through Congress, how they get shelved, how lobbies put the bite on legislators.

Interviewer: Does that have a healthy effect?

COOKE: I hope so—though ignorance was more blissful because you kept your ideals.

Interviewer: What positive things have you noted about TV's influence on U.S. society?

COOKE: Well, as I've implied, it gives people an enormously wider knowledge of the way our society is governed. Certainly, we have seen the face of injustice and of crime and of poverty in ways that unimaginative people would never have picked up from newspaper reports. In this way, the medium itself is a means of great reporting: You see a mother break down; you see a miner's miserable village. It forces you to take in more than you would ever care to read.

Interviewer: Was that the case with the Vietnam war—that people began to get an immediate and vivid idea of war?

COOKE: Yes. Vietnam was, to put it cold-bloodedly, the most interesting example of a general change in the attitude to war itself. I suggested earlier that maybe the change leads to very sloppy conclusions, such as that because war itself is hideous, all wars are useless. If we'd believed that 30 years ago, the States would now be run by *Gauleiters* (that is, district leaders of the Nazi Party).

Let's suppose you'd had television in 1916, and you had John Chancellor, Walter Cronkite, and Howard K. Smith reporting the battles of the Somme: "Tonight the second battle of the Somme continues, and the British estimate their losses today at 60,000. The Germans' are estimated at 80,000. And now a message." Then on the next night they'd come on and say: "This is the third night of the battle of the Somme. Today's count of British casualties is 62,000." I believe there'd have been wholesale revolutions.

The point about Vietnam is that for the first time we had uncensored reporting from the field of battle. We didn't have much detail about the First World War when I was a little boy until the literature came out *after* the war. The reporting of Vietnam came out every day the war was on. We heard a great deal from men on our side who didn't know what they were fighting for and hated the war and were "agin" the Government. This is totally new in the human experience and, of course, from the military point of view, very corrosive of morale.

Interviewer: Doesn't this fact handicap a free society in competing with totalitarian societies?

COOKE: Absolutely. We never saw it better than in the reporting of Vietnam. We saw the agony and the waste and corruption. Every night we saw rickety children or wounded grandmothers and soldiers on litters—and men totally bored with the whole thing. (The whole truth can be a very demoralizing thing.)

The question is: Can we cope with the whole truth when we know that the Russians and the Chinese learn only what their Governments want them to know? In a way, this freedom is our pride, but it's also our agony. And television magnifies it enormously.) Censorship controlled what we knew about the First World War and the Second. Suppose we had seen a two-hour piece, filmed from helicopters and from the ground, on our destruction of Dresden. What would that have done to people?

Interviewer: In that perspective, is this really a much more violent time than we've known in the past?

COOKE: We've not had anything like 1919 [Chicago racial clashes] or the violence in Detroit in 1943, which was the only thing I've seen that could be really called a race riot. When the Southern whites moved up to Willow Run to work in defense production and the blacks started to move into the shabby neighborhoods that the whites occupied, that was murder for two days.

It's too simple to say that violence is worse than it's ever been. The point is that we *know* about it.

I once spent a week or so studying what happened in the spring of one year, 1926, that I had always looked back on nostalgically. I looked at what was happening all over Europe and the British Isles—anything that undoubtedly would have been featured in the evening news. It was a nightmare: famine in India, unemployment riots in Germany, Armenians starving, Britain paralyzed by a general strike, France fighting in Morocco, an army mutiny brewing in Spain.

You read about these things only if you wanted to. Now we see it all happen on television.

Interviewer: Does that give TV newsmen too much power?

COOKE: I think their power is inherent in the medium. There is no way out. The moment you put a man on the screen and he talks to you for 10 minutes, he has enormous power—as much power as his talent can command.

Interviewer: TV commentators are accused of lacking objectivity. Is that a just complaint?

COOKE: I don't think so. Of course, it should be the pride of a network to try to be totally objective, but one problem is that it's not very dramatic to be objective. Maybe your rating will go down. And the networks are just as interested in selling things through their news programs as they are on any other program.

Interviewer: How much has TV lived up to its cultural promise?

COOKE: Frankly, I think wonderfully well. If the Elizabethans had had drama fed to them from 6 a.m. till 2 a.m., Shakespeare would have been through in a week. It's no good saying television's material is rarely first-rate. There isn't that amount of first-rate writing or first-rate thinking in the whole world to keep networks going 24 hours a day. What you can say is that there's too much television time in our society. Television ought to start about 6 p.m.

You haven't asked me, but I will tell you this: It's striking to me that if you live in a small village or a provincial town in England, the general quality of what you see will be much better than the general quality of what you will see if you live in a small town in Utah or Mississippi. But you'll get a far greater range of programming in New York than you will in London. The best British documentaries are done with much more care and, I think, are technically and creatively better. But when it comes to public affairs and exposing the conflicts of the nation's political and social life, I think we do better than anybody.

Once you start traveling around this country, the situation becomes fairly abysmal because you very often find only one or two network affiliates in a town, which means that on Saturday you get basketball or ice hockey, and that's it. The local programs are very badly done indeed—sometimes just imitations of network gossip shows.

But in New York I can't keep up with the things I'd like to see on television. I think I'm even more astounded when I'm there at the quantity of first-rate material that the public broadcasting system puts out.

Interviewer: Do you think that this fall-off in quality when you get away from New York is because of the size of the country compared with Britain?

COOKE: That's the point. I should have said that. It's why, for instance, the British tend to be very "down the nose" about American newspapers when they get away from the East Coast. They forget that they live in a tiny country the size of New York State and a little bit of Pennsylvania. Therefore, they can read *The Times* and *The Telegraph* and *The Guardian* no matter where they live, whereas in this country there are thousands of towns where you can't read *The Los Angeles Times* or *The New York Times,* and you're stuck with your own little paper.

Looking Ahead

Interviewer: As you look down the road, what difference in American life will TV play in the future?

COOKE: Well, we know, for instance, that it's been an enormous help in closed-circuit teaching operations. A lot of teaching, I think, is going to be done by remote control—by good teachers instead of incompetent teachers. This may not be very good for the teaching profession, but in all the sciences, especially in medicine, it's a marvelous thing.

Interviewer: What do you see ahead in television's effect in other ways—in the way we talk, for instance?

COOKE: The thing that alarms me is that you can pick up bad habits more quickly from television than from anything else. I notice children really picking up the butchery of the English language from television, and especially from advertising prose. "Genteelisms" are absolutely riddling the language. I mean, people don't ever moisten their lips any more; they "moisturize." It doesn't rain in Chicago; we now have "precipitation activity in the Chicago area."

As a result of Madison Avenue and the Pentagon, nobody's ever going to be able to read the first chapter of Genesis. "Let there be light" will have absolutely no meaning. I heard a Defense Department official the other evening, and what he wanted to say was that we must be able to attack where we choose. But he didn't say that; he said he was going to "preserve our targeting options."

I hear children talking about "dentifrice." They don't know what toothpaste is.

Interviewer: Are Americans becoming more cynical as they view television and the extravagant promises it proclaims?

COOKE: Yes, yes, I think so. This is an open society, and whether you like it or not, it does encourage cynicism. It makes demands on the maturity and judgment of the individual that are more severe than any he ever had to meet when he had only the press to ponder.

Interviewer: Does this help make us a nation of spectators?

COOKE: Well, that brings us down to something no man can gauge—which is the general morale of the country. If we're a mature people, and we know what our freedom is about, and we remain aware that this great choice of opinion is a good thing, then we're free to make our own judgment without bitterness or hate.

But many people give up and slump into cynicism. And in the end, it comes down to our educational system, especially primary education. If the mass of the people are crudely, badly educated, they will soon give up their liberties for bread and circuses.

In the recently released "Study of Violence in Television: The Industry Looks at Itself," by Thomas F. Baldwin and Colby Lewis of Michigan State University, a TV writer explained "four possible areas of conflict for writers to treat." Most revealing are the comments that follow each category. Here's what he said:

"Man against nature. This is usually too expensive for TV.

"Man against God. Too intellectual for TV.

"Man against himself. Too psychological and doesn't leave enough room for action.

"Man against man. This is what you usually end up with."

Researchers Baldwin and Lewis add: "When men are in conflict and when physical jeopardy is needed to produce excitement, the result is violence or the threat of violence."

HOW TO TELL GOOD GUYS FROM BAD GUYS

JOHN STEINBECK

Television has crept upon us so gradually in America that we have not yet become aware of the extent of its impact for good or bad. I myself do not look at it very often except for its coverage of sporting events, news, and politics. Indeed, I get most of my impressions of the medium from my young sons.

Whether for good or bad, television has taken the place of the sugar-tit, soothing syrups, and the mild narcotics parents in other days used to reduce their children to semiconsciousness and consequently to semi-noisiness. In the past, a harassed parent would say, "Go sit in a chair!" or "Go outside and play!" or "If you don't stop that noise, I'm going to beat your dear little brains out!" The present-day parent suggests, "Why don't you go look at television?" From that moment the screams, shouts, revolver shots, and crashes of motor accidents come from the loudspeaker, not from the child. For some reason, this is presumed to be more relaxing to the parent. The effect on the child has yet to be determined.

I have observed the physical symptoms of television-looking on children as well as on adults. The mouth grows slack and the lips hang open; the eyes take on a hypnotized or doped look; the nose runs rather more than usual; the backbone turns to water and the fingers slowly and methodically pick the designs out of brocade furniture. Such is the appearance of semiconsciousness that one wonders how much of the "message" of television is getting through to the brain. This wonder is further strengthened by the fact that a television-looker will look at anything at all and for hours. Recently I came into a room to find my eight-year-old son Catbird sprawled in a chair, idiot slackness on his face, with the doped eyes of an opium smoker. On the television screen stood a young woman with ice-cream hair listening to a man in thick glasses and a doctor's smock.

"What's happening?" I asked.

Catbird answered in the monotone of the sleep-talker which is known as television voice, "She is asking if she should dye her hair."

"What is the doctor's reaction?"

"If she uses Trutone it's all right," said Catbird. "But if she uses ordinary or adulterated products, her hair will split and lose its golden natural sheen. The big economy size is two dollars and ninety-eight cents if you act now," said Catbird.

You see, something was getting through to him. He looked punch-drunk, but he was absorbing. I did not feel it fair to interject a fact I have observed—that natural golden sheen does not exist in nature. But I did think of my friend Elia Kazan's cry of despair, and although it is a digression I shall put it down.

We were having dinner in a lovely little restaurant in California. At the table next to us were six beautiful, young, well-dressed American girls of the age and appearance of magazine advertisements. There was only one difficulty with their perfection. You couldn't tell them apart. Kazan, who is a primitive of a species once known as men, regarded the little beauties with distaste, and finally in more sorrow than anger cried, "It's years since I've seen or smelled a dame! It's all products, Golden Glint, l'Eau d'Eau, Butisan, Elyn's puff-adder cream—I remember I used to like how women smelled. Nowadays it's all products!"

End of digression.

Just when the parent becomes convinced that

his child's brain is rotting away from television, he is jerked up in another direction. Catbird has corrected me in the Museum of Natural History when I directed his attention to the mounted skeleton of a tyrannosaur. He said it was a brontosaurus but observed kindly that many people made the same error. He argued with his ten-year-old brother about the relative cleanness of the line in Praxiteles and Phidias. He knows the weight a llama will bear before lying down in protest, and his knowledge of entomology is embarrassing to a parent who likes to impart information to his children. And these things he also got from television. I knew that he was picking up masses of unrelated and probably worthless information from television, incidentally the kind of information I also like best, but I did not know that television was preparing him in criticism and politics and that is what this piece is really about.

I will have to go back a bit in preparation. When television in America first began to be a threat to the motion-picture industry, that industry fought back by refusing to allow its films to be shown on the home screens. One never saw new pictures, but there were whole blocks of the films called Westerns which were owned by independents and these were released to the television stations. The result is that at nearly any time of the day or night you could find a Western being shown on some television station. It was not only the children who saw them. All of America saw them. They are a typically American conception, the cowboy picture. The story never varies and the conventions are savagely adhered to. The hero never kisses a girl. He loves his horse and he stands for right and justice. Any change in the story or the conventions would be taken as an outrage. Out of these films folk heroes have grown up—Hopalong Cassidy, the Lone Ranger, Roy Rogers, and Gene Autry. These are

more than great men. They are symbols of courage, purity, simplicity, honesty, and right. You must understand that nearly every American is drenched in the tradition of the Western, which is, of course, the celebration of a whole pattern of American life that never existed. It is also as set in its form as the *commedia dell' arte*.

End of preparation.

One afternoon, hearing gunfire from the room where our television set is installed, I went in with that losing intention of fraternizing with my son for a little while. There sat Catbird with the cretinous expression I have learned to recognize. A Western was in progress.

"What's going on?" I asked.

He looked at me in wonder. "What do you mean, what's going on? Don't you know?"

"Well, no. Tell me!"

He was kind to me. Explained as though I were the child.

"Well, the Bad Guy is trying to steal Her father's ranch. But the Good Guy won't let him. Bullet figured out the plot."

"Who is Bullet?"

"Why, the Good Guy's horse." He didn't add "You dope," but his tone implied it.

"Now wait," I said, "which one is the Good Guy?"

"The one with the white hat."

"Then the one with the black hat is the Bad Guy?"

"Anybody knows that," said Catbird.

For a time I watched the picture, and I realized that I had been ignoring a part of our life that everybody knows. I was interested in the characterization. The girl, known as Her or She, was a blonde, very pretty but completely unvoluptuous because these are Family Pictures. Sometimes she wore a simple gingham dress and sometimes a leather skirt and boots, but always she had a bit of a bow in her hair and her face was untroubled with emotion or, one might almost say, intelligence. This also is part of the convention. She is a symbol, and any acting would get her thrown out of the picture by popular acclaim.

The Good Guy not only wore a white hat but light-colored clothes, shining boots, tight riding pants, and a shirt embroidered with scrolls and flowers. In my young days I used to work with cattle, and our costume was blue jeans, a leather jacket, and boots with run-over heels. The cleaning bill alone of this gorgeous screen cowboy would have been four times what our pay was in a year.

The Good Guy had very little change of facial expression. He went through his fantastic set of adventures with no show of emotion. This is another convention and proves that he is very brave and very pure. He is also scrubbed and has an immaculate shave.

I turned my attention to the Bad Guy. He wore a black hat and dark clothing, but his clothing was definitely not only unclean but unpressed. He had a stubble of beard but the greatest contrast was in his face. His was not an immobile face. He leered, he sneered, he had a nasty laugh. He bullied and shouted. He looked evil. While he did not swear, because this is a Family Picture, he said things like "Wall dog it" and "You rat" and "I'll cut off your ears and eat 'em," which would indicate that his language was not only coarse but might, off screen, be vulgar. He was, in a word, a Bad Guy. I found a certain interest in the Bad Guy which was lacking in the Good Guy.

"Which one do you like best?" I asked.

Catbird removed his anaesthetized eyes from the screen. "What do you mean?"

"Do you like the Good Guy or the Bad Guy?"

He sighed at my ignorance and looked back at the screen. "Are you kidding?" he asked. "The Good Guy, of course."

Now a new character began to emerge. He puzzled me because he wore a gray hat. I felt a little embarrassed about asking my son, the expert, but I gathered my courage. "Catbird," I asked shyly, "what kind of a guy is that, the one in the gray hat?"

He was sweet to me then. I think until that moment he had not understood the abysmal extent of my ignorance. "He's the In-Between Guy," Catbird explained kindly. "If he starts bad he ends good and if he starts good he ends bad."

"What's this one going to do?"

"See how he's sneering and needs a shave?" my son asked.

"Yes."

"Well, the picture's just started, so that guy is going to end good and help the Good Guy get Her father's ranch back."

"How can you be sure?" I asked.

Catbird gave me a cold look. "He's got a gray hat, hasn't he? Now don't talk. It's about time for the chase."

There it was, not only a tight, true criticism of a whole art form but to a certain extent of life itself. I was deeply impressed because this simple explanation seemed to mean something to me more profound than television or Westerns.

Several nights later I told the Catbird criticism to a friend who is a producer. He has produced many successful musical comedies. My friend has an uncanny perception for the public mind and also for its likes and dislikes. You have to have if you produce musical shows. He listened and nodded and didn't think it was a cute child story. He said, "It's not kid stuff at all. There's a whole generation in this country that makes its judgments pretty much on that basis."

THE "LATE SHOW" CLICHÉ MOVIE SCRIPT

The "Swashbuckler" Movie

The people grow more restless each day, my Queen. They say they are being taxed beyond endurance!

Bring this rascal to me at once. I'd like to see for myself who held off de Roquefort's special guards single-handedly...this, what do they call him...this "Golden Hawk!"

Your enemies are not out there, your Highness, but here in your own court! They use their office not for the good of the people, but for personal wealth and gain!

Say the word, your Highness, and I'll pluck the feathers from this "Golden Hawk!"

No, let him speak, Baron. His tongue lacks respect, but his courage must be commended. If only he'd put it to use for the crown rather than against it!

We strike tonight while everyone is at the wedding ceremony of Princess Suzanne. I know a secret tunnel to the palace shown to me by my father when he was Keeper of the Royal Forest for King Waldo!

I'm sorry, my child, but you must go through with this wedding with Count Varnoff. I know the Count is not young, nor thin, nor handsome — but these are the dreams of foolish girls, not Princesses.

. . . .

Wait, my Queen! Before you sign that marriage certificate! I bring proof of de Roquefort's treachery! From the very beginning he and Count Varnoff have been conspiring against you and your plans to free our people from this slavery they now suffer!

. . . .

Does the Queen believe the word of this son of a forest keeper or a Baron?

. . . .

I speak no more, Varnoff! My sword speaks for me! En Garde!

. . . .

Varnoff and de Roquefort — two of the best swordsmen in Europe! The Golden Hawk is no match for them! We must go to his aid ...

. . . .

Leave him be! I raised the Hawk from when he was a young pup. He'll give them both a lesson in swordplay!

. . . .

You have won the gratitude of your Queen along with the hearts of her people, Golden Hawk. And if this old woman's eyes prove correct, you have won the heart of Princess Suzanne as well. Certainly you will be able to make her a comfortable bride now that you are Keeper of the Royal Forest!

. . . .

To serve my Queen is the only reward I ask!

THE END

THE "LATE SHOW" CLICHÉ MOVIE SCRIPT

THE "POLITICAL" MOVIE

"I'll be frank, Professor Woodrow—we've come to you because you're the only man we can trust. With you in the Governor's chair, we can clean up this State and make it a decent place in which to live and bring up our children."

"What do you say, Louise? It's up to you. It means giving up the University and all the other things we'd planned to do."

"No Dave! I refuse to make any deals! If I'm going to be Governor of this State, I've got to run things my way! Now tell Brady to get out of here, and take his votes with him!"

"You know, Professor, I'm beginning to think you're sincere about all this reform business! And I thought this lady reporter's eyes had seen everything!"

"Politics is a dirty business, Professor. You can't help getting a little mud on yourself. Just remember this...it didn't stop Abe Lincoln!"

"I was so proud of that speech you made tonight, Mark. Everyone's talking about it."

"I learned something today, Louise, that almost made me lose faith. Senator Cartwright, my life-long idol, is no better than the others. He offered me half a million dollars to sink the Flood Control Bill. I threw him out of my office."

"It looks bad, Mark. Finchley's dug up that old scandal, and he's out to play it up for all it's worth."

"I don't mind for myself, Louise. It's just that I hate to see you and the children dragged into a mess like this."

"Yes, ladies and gentlemen, it's true! I did serve time on a chain gang—for a crime I did not commit! And now, with your permission, I'd like to withdraw my name as a candidate for Governor of this State . . ."

"No! No! No! We want Woodrow! We want Woodrow!!"

"Hear that, Mark? They want you! They still want you!!"

"We've got a big job ahead of us, Louise—but with His help, we'll see it through!"

THE END

THE "LATE SHOW" CLICHÉ MOVIE SCRIPT

THE "SOCIETY" MOVIE

"I don't know what's gotten into Pamela lately. The girl seems to have lost all sense of propriety. Yesterday, I caught her dancing with the Chauffeur. Imagine that, Laureen! The Chauffeur!"

"If you must know, Mother, I'm fed up with this life you seem to think is so wonderful. I'm especially fed up with all these useless, empty people who think happiness can be bought with a bank account."

"Pamela, your mother and I have decided. We're shipping you off to Europe tomorrow. When you've had a few weeks in the sun at Monte Carlo, you'll come to your senses and forget all about this 'taxi-cab' person."

"Perhaps we've handled this thing all wrong, Laureen. I think it's a *good* idea to invite this young man to the ball. When she sees how out of place he is among all this, perhaps Pamela will forget that insane idea of hers about moving to Brooklyn."

". . . and did you see those dreadful people he brought with him? I understand they're his parents! I can't imagine why George and Laureen would permit such a thing!"

"You needn't worry, Mrs. Smythe-Wellborne, I'll not contaminate your home with my bourgeois presence any longer. As for the check, my feelings for Pamela have no price tag. You couldn't buy them with ALL your millions! Well, how about it, Funny-Face? Are you coming with me?"

"I don't know, Joe. I need some time . . . to think . . ."

. . . .

"Now, now, my little girl. Trust your wise old father just this once. I've lived many more years than you and I know. Someday, you'll be grateful that you made this decision. And as a special surprise for you, I've invited Freddy Van Cleef down for the week-end."

. . . .

"There are more important things in life than polo, Freddy. But I don't expect you to understand that. Now, if you'll excuse me, I have an important phone call to make — to a HUMAN BEING — with feelings and emotions. I only hope that he'll talk to me after all the hurt I've caused him."

. . . .

"I was praying you'd say that, Pam. It may be rough going at first. You won't have furs and diamonds and servants. But I can promise you one thing: you'll always have my love. Think you can live on that, Honey?"

. . . .

"Just try me, Darling!"

. . . .

"You know, Laureen, now that I've gotten to know the lad, I find that I like him. He's got some of that old spark—that 'take it with your bare hands' attitude I once had. Maybe we can all learn a thing or two from him. Anyway, that's why I've decided that he's the man to take over my entire organization!"

THE END

There are 60 million homes in the United States and over 95 percent of them are equipped with a television set. (More than 25 percent have two or more sets.) In the average home the television is turned on some five hours forty-five minutes a day. The average male viewer, between his second and sixty-fifth year, will watch television for over 3000 entire days—roughly nine full years of his life. During the average weekday winter evening nearly half of the American people are to be found silently seated with fixed gaze upon a phosphorescent screen.

Americans receive decidedly more of their education from television than from elementary and high schools. By the time the average child enters kindergarten he has already spent more hours learning about his world from television than the hours he would spend in a college classroom earning a B.A. degree.

The academicians, research scientists and critics have been telling us for years of television's impact upon the attitudes and behavior of those who watch it. They cite very persuasive statistics to indicate that television's influence has affected, in one way or another, virtually every phenomenon in our present-day society.

GOVERNMENT BY CRISIS

During 1966 and 1967 there was a dramatic upsurge in the amount of rioting and demonstrations in our cities. As Daniel P. Moynihan reminded us all in the NBC program *Summer 1967: What We Learned,* "We have no business acting surprised at all this. The signs that it was coming were unmistakable." The signs had been reported by those who had been observing, studying and writing about the plight of black Americans. But these warnings were not heard, the crises came, captured our attention, and put us in a mood to listen. The National Advisory Commission on Civil Disorders, better known as the Kerner Commission, was established, conducted a thoroughgoing investigation, and wrote a thoughtful and persuasive report. In this report the Commissioners found it necessary to devote an entire chapter to the mass media. They found themselves confronted at every turn with evidence of the implications of the mass media in a nation wracked with civil disorders. There was not only the matter of the relationship between the reporting of incidents and subsequent action. They also discovered a shocking lack of communication and understanding between blacks and whites in this country. Dr. Martin Luther King had told us very much the same thing: "Lacking sufficient access to television, publications and broad forums, Negroes have had to write their most persuasive essays with the blunt pen of marching ranks."

The Kerner Commission report had no more than found its way to the coffee tables of white suburbia before this nation was torn apart once again—this time with the agonizing, heart-wrenching sorrow accompanying the assassinations of Dr. Martin Luther King and Senator Robert F. Kennedy. Once again a crisis, once again national attention, once again a Commission, the National Commission on the Causes and Prevention of Violence, whose studies inevitably had to confront the evidence of the implications of the mass media. As Dr. Albert Bandura, professor of psychology at Stanford University, has recently said:

It has been shown that if people are exposed to television aggression they not only learn aggressive patterns of behavior, but they also retain them over a long period of time. There is no longer any need to equivocate about whether televised stimulation produces learning effects. It can serve as an effective tutor.

The latest Commission was not even permitted to conclude its deliberations and issue a report before the third in this series of crises hit the American people. It was, of course, the confrontation at Chicago and the Democratic national convention. In this instance the mass media were not only implicated in the confrontation, they were an active party. (In the words of the report "Rights in Conflict" by Daniel Walker: "What 'the whole world was watching,' after all, was not a confrontation but the picture of a confrontation, to some extent directed by a generation that has grown up with television and learned how to use it.")

How many more crises must we undergo before we begin to understand the impact of television upon *all* the attitudes and events in our society? How many more such crises can America withstand and survive as a nation united? Are we going to have to wait for dramatic upturns in the number and rates of high school dropouts, broken families, disintegrating universities, illegitimate children, mental illness, crime, alienated blacks and young people, alcoholism, suicide rates and drug consumption? Must we blindly go on establishing national commissions to study each new crisis of social behavior as if it were a unique symptom unrelated to the cause of the last? I hope not.

Of course, no one would suggest that television is the *only* influence in our society. But it is time for all in responsible positions to have both the perception and the courage to say what is by now so obvious to many of the best students of American society in the 1970's. Television *is* a common in-

gredient in a great many of the social ills that are troubling Americans so deeply today and we ought to know much more about it than we do. One cannot understand violence in America without understanding the effect of television programming upon that violence. But one cannot understand the impact of television programming upon violence without coming to grips with the ways in which television influences virtually all of our attitudes and behavior.

Whenever the question arises of the effect of television programming upon the attitudes and behavior of the audience, industry spokesmen are likely to respond with variants of three myths:

1 We just give the people what they want. "The public interest is what interests the public." The viewer must be selective, just as he would be in selecting magazines. He gets to choose from the great variety of television programming we offer. He can always turn off the set.

2 Entertainment programming doesn't have any impact upon people. It's just entertainment. We can't be educational all the time.

3 We report the news. If it's news we put it on; if it's not we don't. It's as simple as that. We can't be deciding what to put on the news or not based upon its impact upon public opinion or national values. We can't be held responsible if someone sees something on television and goes out and does the same thing.

THE MYTH OF SERVING PUBLIC TASTE

By and large broadcasting today is run by corporations which have a virtual lease in perpetuity on the right to broadcast. These corporations are like all other businesses; they are interested in maximizing their profits. The market value of their business, including the right to broadcast, is directly related to the profits the business returns. And this value can be realized in a virtually free market for the purchase and sale of established stations. This is not to be viewed as a hostile judgment of these men and corporations. America has been served well by the profit motive in a competitive system. It does suggest, however, that the system today is different from that envisioned by those who molded the present regulatory framework.

But we must examine the economic incentives as well. Broadcasters act to gain as large an audience as possible—and the audience is attracted by the broadcasters' programming. Programming is chosen for the number of people it can deliver. Its selection need not reflect the intensity of the audience's approval, or what the audience would be willing to pay for the programming. In fact, the incentive to get the largest audience regardless of good taste has on occasion driven the networks to arrogant indifference to "what the public wants." The Dodd Committee report refers to an incident in which an independent testing organization conducted an advance audience reaction test of an episode from a network series show. Of the men, women and children tested, 97 percent believed there was too much emphasis on sex, and 75 percent felt the show was unsuitable for children. The network ignored the findings, and televised the episode.

To say that current programming is what the audience "wants" in any meaningful sense is either pure doubletalk or unbelievable naiveté. There are many analytical problems with the shibboleth that television "gives the people what they want." One of the most obvious is that the market is so structured that only a few can work at "giving the people what they want"—and oligopoly is a notoriously poor substitute for competition when it comes to providing anything but what the vast majority will "accept" without widespread revolution.

This is not to suggest that stations and networks engage exclusively in profit-maximizing behavior —only that this is the predominant component of their business motivation. And, I repeat, I am not now passing moral judgment on this behavior. I am simply pointing out that this is the system we have created, and that it is significantly different from the one that was envisioned forty years ago.

Stations and networks sometimes do engage in programming that is not the most profitable available to them. Thus, Justice Black was permitted to speak to some ten million Americans in December 1968 on CBS. The concern of CBS was not only whether its relatively low programming costs were covered by the commercial revenue from that program (there were eight products or services advertised), but the "opportunity cost" in the form of *additional* return CBS might have obtained from regular programming aimed at a larger audience. (Networks are also concerned about losing audience on the shows to follow, since there is some viewer carryover from program to program—another force that has precluded advertisers from sponsoring public service shows of their own choosing, even when they are willing to pay handsomely for the opportunity). Of course, there are many responsible individuals, associated with stations and networks alike, who realize the great power of this medium for good and who try to use it. The point is simply that each of them is limited by the functioning of the system—a system that doesn't allow significant deviation from the goal of profit maximizing. Some have left commercial broadcasting because of that constraint.

It should be clear why attempts to affect the quality of programming have often focused on changing the rules of the system. Shouting exhortations at an edifice is a poor substitute for some structural changes. Proposals have been designed to open up the program procurement process, to restructure the affiliate-network relationship, to increase the number of TV stations, and to make rules concerning the types of programming to be presented. Educational broadcasting—as well as the potential of subscription television and cable television—are fundamental responses to the functioning of the present commercial system.

THE MYTH OF LACK OF IMPACT

The argument that television entertainment programming has no impact upon the audience is one of the most difficult for the broadcasting industry to advance. In the first place, it is internally self contradictory. Television is sustained by advertising. It is able to attract something like $2.5 billion annually from advertisers on the assertion that it is the most effective advertising medium. And it has, in large measure, delivered on this assertion. There are merchandisers, like the president of Alberto Culver, who are willing to say that "the investment will virtually always return a disproportionately large profit." Alberto Culver has relied almost exclusively on television advertising and has seen its sales climb from $1.5 million in 1956 to $80 million in 1964. The manufacturer of the bottled liquid cleaner Lestoil undertook a $9 million television advertising program and watched his sales go from 150,000 bottles annually to 100 million in three years—in competition with Procter and Gamble, Lever Brothers, Colgate, and others. The Dreyfus Fund went from assets of $95 million in 1959 to $1.1 billion in 1965 and concluded, "TV works for us." American industry generally has supported such a philosophy with investments in television advertising increasing from $300 million in 1952 to $900 million in 1956 to $1.8 billion in 1964 to on the order of $2.5 billion in 1968. Professor John Kenneth Galbraith, in the course of surveying *The New Industrial State,* observes that, "The industrial system is profoundly dependent upon commercial television and could not exist in its present form without it. . . . [Radio and television are] the prime instruments for the management of consumer demand."

The sociologist Peter P. Lejins describes four studies of the effect upon adult buying of advertising directed at children. Most showed that on the order of 90 percent of the adults surveyed were asked by children to buy products, and that the child influenced the buying decision in 60 to 75 percent of those instances. Dr. Lejins observes, "If the advertising content has prompted the children to this much action, could it be that the crime and violence content, directly interspersed with this advertising material, did not influence their motivation at all?" There is, of course, much stronger evidence than this of the influence of violence in television programming upon the aggressive behavior of children which I will discuss later. The point is, though, that television's salesmen cannot have it both ways. They cannot point with pride to the power of their medium to affect the attitudes and behavior associated with product selection and consumption, and then take the position that everything else on television has no impact whatsoever upon attitudes and behavior.

Our evidence of commercial television's influence is not by any means limited to the advertising. Whatever one may understand Marshall McLuhan to be saying by the expression "the medium is the message," it is clear that television has affected our lives in ways unrelated to its program content. Brooklyn College sociologist Dr. Clara T. Appell reports that of the families she has studied 60 percent have changed their sleep patterns because of television, 55 percent have changed their eating schedules, and 78 percent report they use television as an "electronic babysitter." Water system engineers must build city water supply systems to accommodate the drop in water pressure occa-

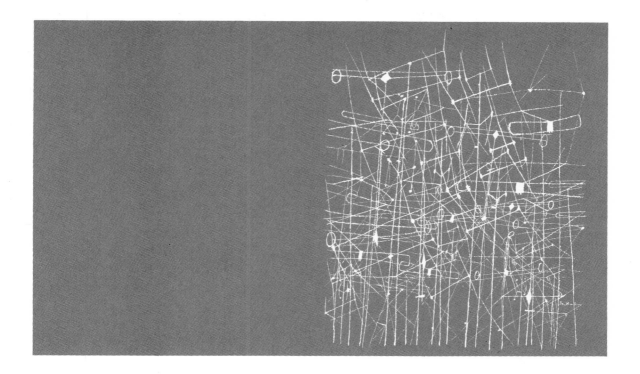

sioned by the toilet-flushing during television commercials. Medical doctors are encountering what they call "TV spine" and "TV eyes." Psychiatrist Dr. Eugene D. Glynn expresses concern about television's "schizoid-fostering aspects," and the fact that "it smothers contact, really inhibiting interpersonal exchange." General semanticist and San Francisco State president Dr. S. I. Hayakawa has observed that television snatches children from their parents for 22,000 hours before they are eighteen, giving them little "experience in influencing behavior and being influenced in return." He asks, "Is there any connection between this fact and the sudden appearance . . . of an enormous number of young people . . . who find it difficult or impossible to relate to anybody—and therefore drop out?"

A casual mention on television can affect viewers' attitudes and behavior. When television's Daniel Boone, Fess Parker, started wearing coonskin caps, so did millions of American boys. The sales of Batman capes and accessories are another, albeit short-lived, example.

Television establishes national speech patterns and eliminates dialects, not only in this country but around the world—"Tokyo Japanese" is now becoming the standard throughout Japan. New words and expressions are firmly implanted in our national vocabulary from television programs—such as Rowan and Martin's "Sock it to me," or Don Adams's "Sorry about that, Chief." Television can even be used to encourage reading. The morning after the late Alexander King appeared on the late-night Jack Paar show his new book, *Mine Enemy Grows Older,* was sold out all over the country. When the overtly "educational" Continental Classroom atomic age physics course began on network television 13,000 textbooks were sold the first week.

Politicians evidently think television is influential. Most spend over half of their campaign budgets on radio and television time—$59 million in 1968—and some advertising agencies advise that virtually all expenditures should go into television. When Sig Mickelson was president of CBS News he commented on "television's ability to create national figures almost overnight . . ."—a phenomenon which by now we have all witnessed.

Indeed, as Bradley S. Greenberg of Michigan State reported to the Violence Commission: "Forty percent of the poor black children and 30 percent of the poor white children (compared with 15 percent of the middle-class white youngsters) were ardent believers of the true-to-life nature of the television content." And he went on to further underline the "educational" impact of all television

Eleven of the reasons for watching television dealt with the ways in which TV was used to learn things—about one's self and about the outside world. This was easy learning. This is the school-of-life notion—watching TV to learn a lot without working hard, to get to know all about people in all walks of life, because the programs give lessons for life, because TV shows what life is really like, to learn from the mistakes of others, etc. The lower-class children are more dependent on television than any other mass medium to teach these things. They have fewer alternative sources of information about middle-class society, for example, and therefore no competing or contradictory information. Thus, the young people learn about the society that they do not regularly observe or come in direct contact with through television programs—and they believe that this is what life is all about.

Knowing these things, as by now all television executives must, they must expect society to hold them to extremely high standards of responsibility.

Do we impose these standards on them? Consider, before you answer, what we learn about life from television. Watch for yourself, and draw your own conclusions. Here are some of my own. We learn that the great measure of happiness and personal satisfaction is consumption—conspicuous when possible. "Success" is signified by the purchase of a product—a mouthwash or deodorant. How do you resolve conflicts? By force and by violence. Who are television's leaders, its heroes, its stars? They are the physically attractive, the glib, and the wealthy, and almost no one else. What do you do when life fails to throw roses in your hedonistic path? You get "fast, fast, fast" relief from a pill—headache remedy, a stomach settler, a tranquilizer, or a pep pill. You smoke a cigarette, have a drink, or get high on pot or more potent drugs. You get a divorce or run away from home. And if, "by the time you get to Phoenix," you're still troubled, you just "chew your little troubles away."

I think it is fair to ask what these network executives are doing. What is this America they are build-

ing? What defense is there for the imposition of such standards upon 200 million Americans? What right has television to tear down every night what the American people are spending $52 billion a year to build up every day through their school system? Giving the people what they want? Nonsense.

THE MYTH OF THE NEWS

Production of news and public affairs programming is, by common agreement, American television's finest contribution. The men who run it are generally professional, able, honorable and hardworking. To the extent the American people know what's going on in the world much of the credit must go to the networks' news teams. It is a tough and often thankless job. These men have fought a good many battles for all of us—with network management, advertisers, government officials, and news sources generally. We are thankful. And, by and large, I think we ought to stay out of their business—with the exception, perhaps, of providing them protection from physical assault. I would not for a moment suggest that a government commission ought to be providing standards for what is reported as "news." Partisan efforts by government to manipulate and intimidate television to propagandize on behalf of a particular candidate, political party, or ideology are simply intolerable in a free society. At the same time, I think that no one need feel under compulsion to avoid any comment whatsoever on the subject.

Whenever one begins discussing the violence quotient in televised news the broadcasting establishment (far more often than the thoughtful newsmen themselves) is apt to come out with something about the First Amendment and journalistic integrity. The implication is that there is some socially desirable, professionally agreed upon definition of "news"—known only to those who manage television stations and networks—which is automatically applied, and that any efforts to be reflective about it might contribute to the collapse of the republic.

My view is simply that this is nonsense, and that the slightest investigation of the product of journalism will demonstrate it to be such. Robert Kintner, a broadcaster of many years, once wrote, "Every reporter knows that when you write the first word you make an editorial judgment." "Education" did not become news until *The New York Times* set up a special Sunday section on it. Whether and how "television" is reported as news in *Newsweek* depends in part upon what they call the sections of the magazine—and those headings change. The same is true of "science" or "medicine." We do not get much meaningful reporting about the federal budget, the choices it represents and the processes by which they were made. We could get more, simply if an editor or a newsman took an interest in the matter.

I would agree with the statement of Reuven Frank, president of NBC News, in *TV Guide* that we benefit from living in a nation with "free journalism," which he defines as "the system under which the reporter demands access to facts and events for no other reason than that he is who he is, and his argument is always accepted." I want the check of the news media upon government officials—including myself. But I do not believe—and he does not suggest—that free journalism need function as irresponsible journalism, completely free of check, comment or criticism from professional critics, a concerned public and responsible officials. Journalists can alter what subjects they report and how they report them—and they do. They can do this in response to a sense of professional responsibility. They often have. I ask no more; we should expect no less.

NICHOLAS JOHNSON

former Federal Communications Commissioner

Television educates us away from life and away from our individuality.
It drives us to line up at the counters of drugstores and supermarkets, shaping
our needs and wants, and ultimately ourselves, into the molds that are the
products. Not only does it explicitly preach conspicuous consumption, status
consciousness, sexploitation and fantasy worlds of quick shallow solutions,
even the settings and subliminal messages are commercials for the
consumption style of life.

I think television could—and should—help us understand the alternatives
to the conspicuous consumption, chemical, corporate life style. Not because
I'm "right," but because there *are* alternatives. People are entitled to know
about them, and to experience them if they choose. And because today's
televised theology seems to be contributing very little to life, or liberty, or the
pursuit of happiness—which somebody once thought *was* the
business of government.

Have the TV Networks Gone Too Far?

Some Differing Opinions

WHITNEY M. YOUNG, JR.

late executive director of the National Urban League

I disagree with those who say that television creates an atmosphere for violence by portraying violence in the shows it presents on the screen.

I think, for example, that people are not being honest and factual and scientific when they attribute the increasing violence in the country to the impact of *Gunsmoke* and other television shows. The increased violence in Harlem is due largely to poverty; to dope and the unwillingness of the Federal government and other officials to crack down on crime syndicates which really control the dope racket from downtown. It is not controlled by the little people of Harlem.

Fifty percent of the crime in Harlem is related to dope. The violence stems from robberies and other crimes by addicts trying to get money to get a fix and not because *Gunsmoke*—or any other show—happens to be on television.

FRANK STANTON

president of the Columbia Broadcasting System

The troubled pages of this century's history are writ dark with the death of liberty in those nations where the first fatal symptom of political decay was an effort to control the news media. Seldom has it been called censorship. Seldom is the word used except in denials. Always it has been "guidelines" in the name of national unity. And we might well ponder the fate of the unhappy role of nations that had no regard for their freedoms or took them for granted or held them lightly.

The game of TV interviewing has certain rules:

gentility,

probe,

payoff for product or person,

wrapup.

The nature of the beast is such that the interviewer cannot really dispute the half-lie, insert facts without seeming impolite, or later add his own interpretation.

These flaws in the spoken process before an audience, live or out there, prevent a real profile from being drawn or a serious arrangement of ideas.

RADIO

LES BROWN

A group of us stranded at an old printing plant in the Bronx learned from a tiny receiver (which happily someone had had in his pocket) that we were not alone in our plight, and once informed of what had gone wrong we patiently waited it out, feeling safe ourselves but concerned with how the blackout was affecting others. We hovered over that little radio, the bunch of us, dependent on its steady dispatches as our only contact with the outside. Radio was a brilliant communicator that night, and undoubtedly because of it there was little hysteria among the affected and surprisingly few casualties of the power failure.

A medium much taken for granted and usually connected in our minds with recordings and chatter demonstrated an inherent superiority over the other media and probably saved hundreds of lives. The portability of radio, the compactness of it, the ease with which it can relay voices from distant points, the speed with which it can deliver news bulletins, its ready adaptability to emergencies, and finally its transcendence of plug-in electricity all came into play, as they had many times in heroic performances elsewhere in the country during calamities.

But commercial radio survives in America as only a faint echo of its old self, although nicely enough as a business. For those who were not alive before there was television, it is well to know what radio used to be, for its real powers are far from realized today. Some day the medium-that-was may be rediscovered. Reflecting on the time when *it* was that magic box in our homes, for twenty-five years before the end of World War II, I find it still anything but backward or primitive.

We spoke then of radio playing in the *theater of the mind*. Through sound and the suggestion of language, radio created images which we, sitting in our living rooms, felt we were seeing. Words could make us smell the cake baking in the oven, and scenery was painted in a phrase. Everything in the theater of the mind was in color and three dimensions.

Radio is far more pervasive now than it ever was, but it is a long way from its golden era when the most popular series ever, "Amos 'n' Andy," all but stopped commerce at seven o'clock each weeknight. During its broadcasts, telephone usage measurably dropped in half across the country, and movie houses, restaurants, and stores stopped everything to play the evening's fifteen-minute episode rather than lose their clientele to a radio set elsewhere.

Today's radio has been shaped by economic realities. It's difficult to adequately measure radio's dispersed, out-of-home audience, and so radio finds it hard to argue for advertising dollars. How do you count radio's audience except by diary and questionnaire—and who can vouch for the accuracy of the method? Most of us are never as conscious of our radio listening as of our TV viewing; often we dial about and settle on a station without knowing its call letters. Sometimes we really listen, and sometimes we merely have the radio on to keep us company but don't pay attention to it. Radio operators cannot know as much about their audience as television operators do.

Largely, a radio station consists of a handful of announcers, or disk jockeys, working in shifts with a library of records. With that as entertainment, the station's normal vital services include time, weather and traffic information (the bigger stations hiring helicopters for their reports), ball scores, and news headlines. Because radio tends to be more a wake-up medium than television (clock radios contributing to tradition), and because those driving to work will use the medium, radio's prime time is in the morning, from six to nine o'clock, and secondarily in the early evening when drivers return from work. When television's prime time begins, around seven o'clock in the evening, most of radio's audience will have left it.

It's interesting to note how radio differs now as a mass medium from its offspring, television. For one thing, while networks dominate television, they scarcely exist in radio anymore except as news services. For another, while television seeks broad and massive audiences and plays to everyone at once, most radio stations content themselves with limited and specific audiences.

With as many as fifty stations on the AM and FM bands serving some of the larger cities, each station specializes for survival, carving out a place for itself by serving a definable portion of the community. Some play rock music for youth, some sweet string-laden recordings for an older audience, some middle-of-the-road (once known as "popular") music presumably for the age group between. Others may confine themselves to country and western, jazz, classical, or folk music; some are black-oriented (and when there are more than one in a market, the black stations break down into specialties of rock, gospel, and rhythm and blues); some are religion-oriented; some feature foreign-language programming; some deal in talk involving telephone call-ins; and, in cities which can support it, some offer only news.

The theory in radio today is that regular listeners want the station to be the same all the time, to maintain the same style, the same pacing, and the same kind of music throughout the day. Thus, if a listener wants rock music any time of the day, he knows where to find it.

The head of an all-news station explained to me once that he envisioned his broadcast service as a utility. He said, "When people want light, they confidently flick the light switch; when they want water, they turn on the tap; and when they want news, they will turn us on."

The success around the country of many stations with rigid formats tends to bear out the theory, although there are still a number of more generalized stations which defy it and which have known extraordinary success with variegated programming, such as WCCO in Minneapolis, WOR in New York, WGN in Chicago, KMOX in St. Louis, and WSB in Atlanta.

Radio stations outnumber television stations eight-to-one in the United States. By early 1973, there were well over seven thousand radio licensees, nearly two thirds of them on the AM (amplitude modulation) band. The total includes some five hundred educational (or public) radio stations, most of them on FM (frequency modulation). As the years pass, the number of stations is bound to swell, for there are still plenty of unclaimed FM frequencies, although most are in the smaller communities where large audiences and sufficient advertising are hard to come by.

The FM band had been expected to boom after World War II, but television eclipsed it. The typical consumer, absorbed in the new medium, seemed ill-disposed to investing in an instrument that would bring him more radio channels when he was losing interest in the existing ones. FM's main selling point was superior sound quality, which had value to lovers of classical music, and for many years it languished as an elite medium with almost a restricted circulation and the merest advertising support. Many pioneers in FM went broke, and the networks so lost interest that they simply duplicated their AM services on FM.

But in the late sixties, FM made a significant

breakthrough resulting from a combination of developments. A number of stations had made a timely switch to rock music just as that form was gaining a kind of cultural status, and the quality of the audio reproduction began to matter with the fans of rock. This corresponded with, and partially inspired, a boom in stereo equipment, including stereo FM tuners, and by 1972 the sale of FM receivers and AM-FM combination sets outpaced the sale of AM-only sets.

The emergence of FM had the effect of fragmenting the listenership to the extent that the new band became competitive with the old, so competitive in fact that in some cities FM stations took the lead over all stations—and the interesting fact here is that most of those that went to the top played not rock but the so-termed middle-of-the-road music. Beyond sound, an inducement to FM listening has been the more moderate advertising policies of those stations as compared with the heavily commercialized AM stations, many of which still devote more than a quarter of every hour to advertisements. At any rate, the flourishing of FM made it useful to speak of both bands together as simply radio.

With so much radio service already, and the availability of still more frequencies, serious thought is being given in government circles to a relative deregulation of the medium, which would free the stations from many if not all of their license obligations. Preliminary steps have in fact been taken, but thus far they have amounted to little more than easing the paper work. Without government regulation (beyond engineering restrictions to keep stations from jamming each other), radio might practice free enterprise in the full sense, like newspapers and magazines. Freed of being forced to serve "the public interest, convenience, and necessity," stations would be left to prosper or fail on their merits in the marketplace. Would that, in your opinion, produce a better or a worse kind of radio service? Would it affect how radio performs in emergencies? What kind of changes do you envision in the medium without regulation?

The decline of the radio networks does not so much parallel the rise of the television networks as it does the trend to specialization in local radio. Because the radio networks served vast numbers of stations they continued to see themselves playing to a broad spectrum of audiences, but as stations turned to single daylong formats and hence to a narrow stripe of the listenership, network programming became a liability rather than an asset. When it became vitally important for a station to have a consistent *sound* throughout the day, the network was so frequently out of key that it defeated what the station was trying to do. For example, during the early sixties rock stations that were affiliated with ABC network had to carry the folksy long-running show, "Don McNeill's Breakfast Club," pleasant enough, but ultra-square to the rock buffs and downright incongruous with what the stations otherwise purported to stand for.

Since radio stations were all becoming specialized in different ways, no network could really provide programs—outside of news and public affairs—that were useful to all or even a majority. Under affiliate pressures, the networks began to withdraw from offering full-fledged programs and pared down their essential service to newscasts, occasional special events, and scattered two- or three-minute featurettes.

ABC radio lit on an ingenious solution late in the sixties when it divided itself into four separate networks, each primarily a news service but presented differently so as to conform to the various prevailing styles of local radio. Thus the ABC Contemporary Network sent out news tailored expressly for rock stations, the ABC Entertainment Network for middle-of-the-road and more generalized stations, the

ABC Information Network for talk and all-news stations, and the ABC FM Network for classical and more subdued rock stations.

The Mutual Broadcasting System followed by creating separate networks for black-oriented stations and Spanish-language stations, in addition to its regular service of news, sports, and special events for the established network.

Most radio network programs are kept short so as to interfere as little as possible with local schedules. A number of large stations have dropped network service in order to fully control the consistency of their style of presentation. While in television the networks play a large part in the success of the stations (and those stations that are not affiliated usually experience difficulty in amassing competitive audiences), the dependency is almost the other way around in radio, although stations still derive a certain distinction in their markets from offering one of the national services.

Radio, as it's practiced today, is cheap to produce. Many stations can operate for a year on what it costs to produce a single half-hour of prime-time television on a network. In most cases, little staff is required. Since most of what is involved is voice, recordings, and/or telephone, three of the principals of the great days of radio—the writer, the musician, and the sound-effects man—are no longer on the radio payrolls.

Theater of the mind has been kept alive in America mainly through radio commercials, many of which are dramatizations utilizing the audio techniques that are related to sight. Tape-recorder hobbyists have also preserved the art.

Radio should be seen as well as heard. Perhaps it will be again someday.

RADIO, once a form of group listening that emptied churches, has reverted to private and individual uses since TV.

RADIO has lost its picture—it did have one—
and its glamour, but it retains
its penetration in households and has extended
it to automobiles and, through transistors,
to the beach, the backyard, the streets,
and the ball park.

NEWSPAPERS

Chicago Daily News

MASTHEAD

EAR

MONDAY, JULY 28, 1975 • 15 CENTS IN CHICAGO AND SUBURBS • 25 CENTS ELSEWHERE ☆☆

©1955 by Field Enterprises Inc.   100th Year, Number 176   36 Pages in 3 Sections

Final markets
Red Streak
Stocks off 6

MAIN HEADLINE

Thousands hail Ford in Poland

RULES

CUT

President Ford gets a hug and a kiss from a small girl after she presented Mrs. Ford with flowers upon the Fords' arrival in Warsaw Monday. (AP)

CUTLINE

2 right-wing cop spy figures quarrel, 1 shot

By David Jackson

A former Legion of Justice member was shot Sunday night during a quarrel with another former member of the right-wing terrorist group in a North Side apartment.

Both men have been linked to police spying activities, which are under grand jury investigation after disclosures by The Daily News.

Jerome Gasior, 25, who has testified twice before a county grand jury investigating spying by Chicago police, was shot once in the right side. He was in good condition in Edgewater Hospital.

Stephen Sedlacko, 27, of Streator, Ill., was charged with aggravated battery and aggravated assault, after the shooting in the apartment of Peggy Klein, 27, of 5906 N. Sheridan Rd., described by police as Sedlacko's girl friend.

Sedlacko was scheduled to testify Monday as a witness for Thomas K. Stewart, 24, who is seeking to overturn his conviction for a 1970 armed robbery at a Cicero church.

In a court hearing last week, Stewart implicated Sedlacko and several Chicago policemen in the armed robbery, for which he had been sentenced to two to eight years in prison. Stewart is also a former Legion of Justice member.

POLICE said Gasior went to Sedlacko's fifth-floor apartment, where the two men had several drinks.

While sitting on a balcony, the men began quarreling, according to police. Several per-

Turn to Page 2, Column 1

Cop spying witness admits lies

By Larry Green

A key witness in the Chicago police spying investigation admitted Monday that he had lied while testifying in a 1971 trial in which he was acquitted of a break-in.

Thomas K. Stewart, 24, made the admission while being questioned at a hearing in which he is seeking a new trial for a robbery in 1970.

Questioning him was attorney Warren Wolfson, who represents Chicago policemen called before a county grand jury investigating the police spy scandal.

Stewart, a former member of the Legion of Justice, admitted lying several times in a 1971 trial in which he was acquitted of charges that he broke into the Young Socialist Alliance office at 180 N. Wacker Dr.

BEFORE ADMITTING his previous perjury, Stewart engaged in this question and answer exchange with Wolfson:

Q. Would you lie under oath to suit your purpose?
A. No sir.

Q. Would you lie under oath

Turn to Page 2, Column 6

Gibron coach of Winds

Former Bear head coach Abe Gibron Monday was named to a similar position with the Chicago Winds of the World Football League. Leo Cahill, general manager of the Memphis Southmen, accepted a similar post with the Winds. Details on Page 25.

Cubs win on homer

Jose Cardenal's tie-breaking two-run homer in the fifth inning, his first in nearly two months, led Bill Bonham and the Cubs to a 4-2 victory over the Montreal Expos Monday.

	1	2	3	4	5	6	7	8	9	R	H	E
Expos	0	0	0	2	0	0	0	0	0	2	6	0
CUBS	2	0	0	2	0	0	0	x	—	4	10	1

AT ARLINGTON

4—Mr. Top Shelf 7.20, 4.20, 3.00; A P Good Pasture 3.60, 3.20; Ruboff 5.00.
5—Cool Perfection 4.20, 2.80, 2.60; Tinsley's Image 3.20, 2.80; Strong Diplomat 5.60.

AT SARATOGA

5—Camelford 17.40, 8.20, 5.80; Yvetot 13.60, 6.40; Specialite 3.80.
6—One On The Aisle 6.20, 4.00, 2.80; Northerly 8.80, 5.20; In The Swing 5.40.

Earlier race results on page 28.

Another blisterer due

Tonight—Fair and warm, low in the mid to upper 60s.
Tuesday—Mostly sunny and hot, high in the low 90s.
Chances of precipitation: Less than 30 per cent. See Page 23.

Amusements	30, 31	Harris	12	Mort	17
Anderson	14	Herguth	5	Nightingale	26
Beeline	18	Horoscope	10	Obituaries	29
Bridge	22	Insight	9	Royko	3
Comics	10	Kilpatrick	12	Sports	25-28
Crossword	22	Kraft	14	TV	33
Deaths	29	Mark	33	Want Ads	20-23
Editorials	12	Maxine	19	Weather	23
Everyday	17-19	Money	31, 32	Zwecker	19

INDEX

For home delivery customer service call 321-3030.

Proud Poles show off Warsaw

By Peter Lisagor
Our Washington Bureau Chief

WARSAW — President Ford arrived here Monday to be greeted by several hundred thousand cheering Poles.

The crowd along the six-mile motorcade route from the airport to the Wilanow Palace, where he and Mrs. Betty Ford

DECK

Now for the supersummit.
An editorial: Page 12.

NEWS BRIEF

are staying, waved paper U.S. and Polish flags in a cordial welcome that was not overly demonstrative.

The President and Polish Communist leader Edward Gierek stood much of the way in a Soviet-made Zil limousine during the drive along new expressways in the Polish capital. Ford had last visited Poland as a congressman in 1959.

IN A TRADITIONAL arrival ceremony at the airport, Gierek told the President that "You will see no ruins of War-

Turn to back page, this section

Turks plan to take over more bases

ANKARA (UPI)

DATELINE

The Turkish government informed the United States Monday that Turkish officers will relieve American commanders of 12 U.S. bases in Turkey on Tuesday, U.S. officials said.

Six of them — four intelligence-gathering installations, a U.S. 6th Fleet navigational aid station and non-NATO activities at Incirlik Airbase in southern Turkey — suspended operations Sunday, the officials said.

THE REMAINING six, small communications installations, will continue to operate under Turkish command, the officials said.

The Turkish government ordered an end to military operations at all but one of the 25 American bases before last Saturday in retaliation for congressional refusal to lift a U.S. ban on arms sales to Turkey.

But the United States, which imposed the ban after Turkey's invasion of Cyprus last summer, said it would take at

Turn to back page, this section

The first day of the Freedom Train visit to Chicago is a success as Chicagoans line up to view the exhibits. (Daily News Photo/John L. Tweedle)

Freedom Train opens here without its star choo-choo

By Charlotte Hunt
and Long Hwa-shu

Mayor Richard J. Daley welcomed the American Freedom Train to Chicago Monday, despite the fact its locomotive was late for the debut.

The 425-ton steam locomotive got as far as La Salle St. Sunday, but was not allowed to complete the trip to the Navy Pier exhibition area because of the poor condition of the track.

The huge engine ran into more trouble Monday as it was being backed up. Two sets of wheels jumped the track at Kinzie and Canal, blocking Canal St. traffic.

Daley toured the rest of the 23-car train and proclaimed it "one of the most fascinating exhibits I have ever seen in my life."

"WE'RE ALL proud of the accomplishments that a mul-

tinational civilization put together nearly 200 years ago," Daley said.

He advised the small crowd of early visitors to "talk to your friends and neighbors and

tell them what a great thing it is."

Daley assured the Freedom Train officials that "the weath-

Turn to Page 2, Column 4

Record tax rate set for suburb

By Dave Canfield

BYLINE

LEAD

Parts of south suburban Chicago Heights Monday set an all-time high for tax rates in suburban Cook County as new tax rates for 10 more townships were announced.

At the same time, suburbs in 5 of the 10 townships covered in the new figures should have

Tables on Page 16

lower tax bills, said Salvatore Pullia, head of the county tax extension department.

The new record high of $10.885 for each $100 of assessed valuation was set in the area of Chicago Heights that includes Elementary School District 163, High School District 227 and the Bloom Twp. Sanitary and Park District.

The previous high, which was set in the same section of Chicago Heights a year ago, was $10.283. The new rate is 60.2 cents higher than a year ago, an increase of 5.85 per cent.

THE FIVE townships in which Pullia predicted lower bills were Northfield, Orland, Proviso, Rich and Thornton.

He said higher bills could be expected in Bloom, Norwood Park, Palos, Stickney and Worth townships.

Most of the new tax rates, which are used to compute 1974 tax bills that are payable in 1975, were up.

THE LARGEST percentage increase, 15.45 per cent, was posted in another section of Chicago Heights that falls within the boundaries of the Elementary School District 170.

In that particular section, Pullia said that tax bills could increase by as much as 13 per cent.

Pullia said that while a number of sections in various town-

Turn to back page, this section

JUMP LINE

Holiday Inn at Wolf Point

By Jay McMullen

A $25-million luxury Holiday Inn hotel will occupy the top 10 floors of the new 25-story Apparel Center on Wolf Point, a developer said Monday.

The 527-room hotel will open in February, 1977, according to Robert E. Thomas Jr., vice president of Management Group, which is overseeing the hotel construction for a group of investors.

ONE OF THE features of the new hotel, according to

building, which will contain 140,200 square feet of exposition facilities on its lower floors, is nearing the 25th floor. Topping out is expected Sept. 22.

The Wolf Point building, on the banks of the Chicago River just northwest of the Loop, is owned by the Kennedy family, owners of the adjacent Merchandise Mart.

The superstructure of the

Thomas, is an atrium extending from the lobby on the 14th floor to the top floor.

The hotel also will contain a cocktail lounge with a view of Wolf Point and seven restaurants. Hotel guests will have free parking in the three-level parking garage on the point.

Thomas also said that the Holiday Inn will be the first hotel in the city to be completely protected against fire by automatic sprinklers.

Finding Your Way Through the Newspaper

If the *ears* don't give you enough news about the storm, look over the *kickers,* scan the *decks,* and check the *cuts.* Like doctors or baseball players, newspaper people have a kind of language of their own. You should know some of these new words before you start talking about newspapers.

As you read the following list of names, with their definitions, check whether the parts they identify are on the *Chicago Daily News* front page.

MASTHEAD

The masthead of a newspaper shouts for attention. It announces such things as

The name of the paper

the city it is published in

the day of the week and the date

the volume number

the number of pages and sections

the price

the number of years the paper has been published

EDITION

Many big newspapers publish more than one version of the paper each day. Look for names such as "Suburban Edition," "Sports Final," "Early Bird Edition." Some papers identify editions with symbols only, such as one, two, or three dots or stars.

EARS

The boxes at each side of the paper's name are called ears. Often one of the ears gives the weather. The other may list the slogan of the paper or state the edition. The ears are part of the masthead.

HEADLINES

The main headline on this sample front page stretches across all eight columns. It leads your eyes across the front page to the right hand column where the major news story is printed. This eight-column headline is called a *banner* or *streamer.* The main headline is not always a banner all the way across the page, but it is always the biggest head on the page.

DECK

A second headline, called a deck, often appears between a head and the story. Sometimes two decks are used.

BYLINE

This line of type tells the name of the reporter who wrote the story. Not every story has a byline.

DATELINE

You can tell where the story was written and sometimes when it was filed (sent) by reading the dateline. The news agency for which the reporter writes may also be given. For example: AP (Associated Press) or UPI (United Press International).

LEAD

The first few sentences of a news story are called the lead. The lead is usually a summary of the event being reported.

MAJOR NEWS STORY

This is the story which the editors feel is the most important at the time the edition goes to press. It gets the biggest headline and is usually found in the right hand column or columns on the page.

ANALYSIS

The editors are telling you that this is not a straight news story. The writer is going to give his opinion about the report. Since the front page is usually reserved for reporting facts rather than opinion, the editor wants you to know that this is an exception.

INDEX

Regular readers want to know where the features they like are printed. Although editors try to print features in the same sections every day, this is not always possible. An index helps you find what you want to read quickly.

NEWS BRIEFS

These are summaries of articles or features on the inside pages.

CUT

Long ago, a woodcut was used to print pictures. Now cut means any kind of illustration, such as a photo, drawing, graph, weather map.

CUTLINE OR CAPTION

The line or lines of type that describe the cut (picture).

FOLD

Editors place the most important stories in the half of the page above the fold. This helps to sell the paper, because it is the only part of the newspaper the buyer can see when the folded paper is on the newsstand.

KICKER

This line of type comes above the headline of a story. But you will see that often it is meant to be read *after* you have read the headline.

RULES

These lines fence off one story from another. Check where the rules are when you get confused about which story goes with which headline.

CONTINUED LINE OR JUMP LINE

In order to get more stories on page one, editors print only the beginnings of most stories there. The rest of the story is printed on less valuable space on inside pages. The continued line tells you the page and the column where you will find it. It is called a jump line for short, because you have to jump across other material to get to the rest of the story.

SUBHEADS

These are put in mainly for looks. A black subhead breaks up a long gray column of type. It also may call attention to an important point in the story.

HOW TO FIND THE NEWS YOU WANT TO READ

Newspapers have signs to help you find what you want to read quickly. Each section of the paper may have a heading telling what that particular section contains. On the front page you will usually find an index which lists all of the features in alphabetical order and tells you what page each is on.

If you want the TV schedule, you look under T in the index. You don't have to keep flipping pages until you see the schedule.

Here are some examples of section heads from various newspapers. Notice that they tell you briefly what that particular section contains.

HOW NEWSPAPER SECTIONS ARE IDENTIFIED

As you can see by looking at these headings, newspapers identify sections in different ways. The following are the three most often used:

Letters: First section is A, second section is B, etc.

> Example: See section head for Cleveland's *The Plain Dealer.*

Numbers. First section is 1, second section is 2, etc.

> Example: See section head for *The New York Times.* Newspapers which use letters and numbers to identify sections may also use titles for each section.

> Example: Section 2 of *The New York Times* is labeled Arts and Leisure.

Titles. First section is always news. The second section usually deals with editorials and analysis of the news. Sections are *not* identified by letters or numbers.

> Example: Section head for the *Chicago Sun-Times.*

HOW NEWSPAPER PAGES ARE NUMBERED

Newspapers number their pages in one of two ways:

By sections. Each section starts with 1.

> Example: A1-20, B1-18, C1-14, etc.

By the whole paper. Pages are numbered as in a book.

> Example: *The Plain Dealer* has 70 pages, the front page is page 1 and the last page is 70.

Working Newsman Reveals
How Newspapers are Put Together

Ben H. Bagdikian of Washington Post Discloses "Ins" and "Outs" of Newspaper Game; Tells It Like It Is.

Only a Fraction of News Events are Reported, says Bagdikian. And Four Out of Five Stories are Never Printed!

It is impossible to calculate the potential number of events in the world that on any given day might interest some consumer of news. No news system can conduct a continuous survey of all the 3.5 billion human beings on earth and their 167 governments. Even in the communications-conscious United States, there is only a microscopic portion reported of the events of some public impact that occur among the usual sources of news, like the 10,000 national associations, 91,000 governmental units, 121,000 schools and colleges, 320,000 churches and 2,500,000 business firms.

There will never be enough professional reporters to record all potential news, since theoretically it would require one observer for every participant in human events. If this unpleasant ratio of half the world reporting the activities of the other half should come about, there would not be enough communications capacity for all the reports to be transmitted. If all the reports could be transmitted, they could not be printed. If they could be printed, the reader would never have the time to look at the results.

Yet, unachievable though it is, this is what the news system attempts every day, condemned to a state of perpetual restlessness because it is committed to an impossible mission. It assigns such observers as it has to the places it thinks most likely to produce noteworthy occurrences, and prints what it can of the results. In the United States this is done mainly through the systems of the printed press: the two major news agencies, Associated Press and United Press International; a number of supplementary services that provide specialized journalism; and the contribution of daily papers feeding selections from their own staffs into the national nets. Broadcasting adds significant and vivid items but in terms of original reporting it is a minor part of the total.

Gatekeeper Most Important Man

The professional at the local hub of this network is a crucial, if obscure, figure, the local newspaper subeditor who stands between the results of the whole reporting system and the reader. He has different titles in different places, perhaps "managing editor" in a small paper, or "news editor" in a slightly larger one. Or "wire editor" because today most news comes into the office on teletype machines leased from the national news distribution agencies that are known in the trade as "wire services." Social scientists have decided to call him "gatekeeper" because he controls which stories will be printed and which go to the wastebasket.

He is an obscure man both to the public and within his own trade. Reporters and correspondents have the glamour of being on the scene and having their names attached to accounts of events. Executive editors and publishers are respected or feared by public figures because they control the organizations that decide which men will remain in the public eye.

The gatekeeper does not attract similar attention, but in some ways he has more unofficial power than reporters and publishers. He decides which of the routine stories that arrive on his desk each day will be seen by the public. And by making these decisions he notifies all others in the system which stories in the future are likely to get printed and which ones it is pointless for them to report.

He is not all-powerful. Decisions on major stories are usually, but not always, made by others. If his decisions are noticeably contrary to the news policy of his editorial or corporate supervisors, he hears about it and usually, but not always, conforms. If his decisions are seen later to be drastically different from those on other papers or broadcasting stations that his organization takes seriously, he may alter his standards. Or he may not.

But the daily avalanche of information that flows into a daily newspaper is so great, and decisions are made so rapidly, that most news stories are committed to print quietly and irreversibly by the gatekeeper acting alone.

Most Stories Never See Print!

Field studies show that typically the gatekeeper receives five stories for every one he puts into the paper. In general, the larger the circulation of the paper, the greater the percentage of stories thrown away, since the larger papers, though they have more space, have even more sources of news. The Washington *Post,* for example, with 500,000 daily circulation, is listed as subscribing to the Associated Press, the United Press International, the Los Angeles Times/Washington Post News Service, Chicago Tribune–New York Daily News Service, Chicago Daily News Service, London Sunday Times Service, Dow-Jones Service, and Reuters News Service. For each of its services, it has one or more teletype machines bringing in news more or less continuously. Most smaller papers subscribe to only one service, either AP or UPI, whose output is received on three or fewer teletype machines.

On most papers studied, the gatekeeper daily scans five times more words and five times more individual stories than he can use. But on larger metropolitan dailies (over 350,000 circulation) he may see ten times more words and seven times more stories than the reader ever sees. What the gatekeeper throws away is generally never knowable to the reader. It is as though the events reported in 80 percent of the stories that arrive in local newsrooms never happened. This is inevitable but it is awesome.

What follows is not a description of the total information intake of a whole newspaper, but only that minority but paramount category known as "straight news." In most of the papers studied, this constituted about 27 percent of the total paper. Advertisements took 54 to 67 percent of the total paper. Of the nonadvertising space, news took from 62 to 86 percent of space, the remainder being sports, financial, and non-news features.

There are other gatekeepers on the paper. Those who handle the flow of advertising into the daily editions are important because, among other things, they determine how much space will be left for news. On almost all papers the advertising department determines total pages to be printed and only after this does news receive its allocation.

The conversion of volume of advertisements into total pages for the day is not simple. Presses print varying combinations of pages. Papers are always issued with an even number of total pages since sheets are printed on both sides. But, because of complications in multiple printing, cutting, and folding that vary from paper to paper, paper size may be increased by two pages in some, in others by four pages, in others by six. Part of this calculation is mechanical, but part of it is financial, since it may not be profitable to increase the size of the paper for a small surplus of advertising. The final decision on number of pages for the day is held off as long as possible in order to print a maximum of ads. Thus, early

in the editing cycle the gatekeeper may be told that he has a certain amount of space for his news, but as the final deadline approaches this may be changed. . . .

For the news gatekeeper this standard procedure creates a condition of continuing chaos.

Ideally, the man selecting news for his community would gather before him the entire collection of news items harvested that day, study them comparatively, and then make his selection of which item is most important, which is of second importance, which is of third, and so forth. Having made those decisions, he would observe the total to see if, aside from the individual value of each story, there is something in the total daily report that relates individual stories to each other. Finally, he would, of course, give special weight to the most recently arrived news since, almost by definition, later news should have a better chance of getting into the paper than earlier news. Then it would all be placed quickly before the reader.

That is not what happens. The editor never sees all the stories before he makes his decisions. At the start of his deciding, he does not know what the total news report will look like, so he cannot preselect items that will give cohesion to the final paper. And the latest news, far from having the greatest chance of getting into the paper, has the least. And after he has made the bulk of his decisions it could be **ten hours** before most of the readers see the results.

Monster Presses *Slow*

To reverse this, two technological developments would be necessary. First, the full news report from which the local editor makes his selection would have to be available to him at the time that he begins to commit his stories to print. This does not happen today because, among other reasons, the machines that transmit news into his office do it slowly and piecemeal.

But, even if the full report were instantly available, the manufacturing process that converts this to print is even slower. The newspaper printing system is an expensive, intricate mechanical beast that, like an ulcer patient, must be fed slowly and steadily throughout the day.

Two mechanical systems are used by daily papers in the United States.

Letterpress, the traditional process, is still used by a majority of papers and all large ones. Its basis is the casting of each individual letter into metal, the revolution in printing that began in Western Europe in about 1450. Johann Gutenberg designed individual metal letters and a way to hold them properly to form sentences. Inked and pressed on paper, they produced the printed page. Gutenberg set type by placing each metal letter by hand in its proper place at the rate of one line a minute. So did everyone else for 430-odd years thereafter.

In 1886 in Baltimore Ottmar Mergenthaler produced a large, ungainly machine to do it faster. As an operator pressed a letter on a keyboard, a mold for the letter fell into place, and when molds for the letters and spaces reached the end of the line, melted hot lead was shot through them to form a casting of the completed line. The cast metal lines, arranged in columns, were carried by hand to a table where they were arranged to form the total page. Mergenthaler's linotype machine cast at the rate of 4.9 lines a minute.

In 1932 the teletypesetter was invented to operate the linecasting machine not by hand but by a perforated paper tape which actuated the keyboard. This raised speeds to 5.6 lines a minute.

In 1960 the computer was put to work removing some of the human judgment in making the paper tape, like deciding when to end a line and how to hyphenate a word. This raised typesetting to fourteen lines a minute.

In five hundred years the speed of setting type had risen from one to fourteen lines a minute, and in many newspaper shops this was considered the end of a typographical upheaval.

For photographs, there is a different but similarly complicated process by which the negative is projected onto a photosensitized metal plate and the image treated with acid to pit the areas selectively so that dark areas have many ink-bearing dots and white areas none.

When the cast letters and photoengraved plates are completed they are assembled to form the printed page. For most of the history of printing, this became the printing surface, successively inked and pressed on sheets of paper. For longer use, the original type and engraving were used as a master, and a papier-mâché form was pressed on the raised metallic letters to form a negative. Laid on its back, this mat was filled with hot lead to make a duplicate printing surface. Attached to a flat plate and daubed with ink, it was pressed down on the sheet of paper, which was then pulled out, folded by hand, and became a newspaper.

After Gutenberg What?

For 350 years the device for making the inked impression on paper was basically the same as the one used by Gutenberg, which was a converted wine press that instead of pushing grape against grape was made to push inked type against paper, and gave the institution of "the press" its name. This produced about one hundred impressions an hour. In 1810 it was attached

to a steam engine, which raised the rate to two hundred impressions an hour; a four-page paper with five hundred subscribers would take ten hours to be printed. In England in the early 1800s Friedrich Koenig invented a rotary press, and after his first machine was demolished by an angry crowd consisting of both management and labor, it was successfully installed in the *Times* of London and produced twenty-four hundred impressions an hour. The four-page paper that formerly took ten hours to be printed could be produced in fifty minutes.

This rotary press required a curved printing surface. This was made by placing the mat in a semicylindrical form, from which a lead casting was made and placed on the rotary press. The process, called stereotyping, could produce identical duplicate plates for multiple impressions of the same page.

This is still the process used on most papers. It still takes from seven to ten hours, reverting to the time lag of 160 years ago, though of course, producing modern American papers of many more pages and in very large numbers.

A different process, offset, was adopted after World War II and is in use in about a quarter of American dailies, all smaller ones. Instead of using cast metal letters and engravings, a photograph is made of the completed page and printed on a thin photosensitive sheet of metal or plastic-coated paper.

Offset produced higher-quality printing. But its chief advantage is its natural partnership with the most important invention in typesetting since Gutenberg.

15,000 Lines a Minute

A new device, instead of casting hot lead to make individual metal letters, uses optics and electronics to project at great speed an image of each letter onto photosensitized paper. It can project these letters in many sizes or styles and for any line length desired, changing each character electronically or through lenses rather than physical movement. In some cases it projects each letter precisely on the page where it will appear in final form. In 1964 the Photon and Mergenthaler companies introduced such a machine that cast eighty lines a minute. in 1966 an RCA device cast eighteen hundred lines a minute. In 1967, a CBS-Mergenthaler Linotron, usable for the moment only for specialized publications, was bought by the U.S. Government Printing Office; it casts fifteen thousand lines a minute.

The Bible, whose letters took Gutenberg five years to set, could now be produced by the Government Printing Office in seventy-seven minutes —once the programmers had created a magnetic tape to instruct the computer how to project the letters onto the page.

The linkage of computers and photocomposition will revolutionize production of all images, whether on the printed page or on the electronic screen. Newspapers will be no exception. But the conversion will not be simple and quick.

For one thing, cumbersome and expensive though they are, the present newspaper procedures are reliable and tested; and offset, which most efficiently uses photocomposition, is not yet perfected for very large papers.

Furthermore, newspapers have a great deal of money invested in their old machinery, as much as $1 million worth for a small daily and more than $25 million worth for a large one. Newspapers are even more loath than most businesses to discard machines that still work. . . .

Machines Favor "Old" News

It is the ultimate technological irony of the news profession that the demands of machines rob men of time to think.

From the moment the gatekeeper arrives at his desk, sometimes fourteen hours before his work will be read, he must begin to feed the cumbersome mechanisms that convert news into print. Because each story he sends out reduces the remaining space, any succeeding story of the same importance has less of a chance of being seen. The machines of the news system are biased in favor of old news.

A 1961 study of twenty-three Wisconsin afternoon dailies' use of Associated Press wire copy showed that the most important single factor in use of stories was their time of delivery. Of all stories received before 8 A.M., 49 percent were used; between 8 and 10 A.M., 44 percent; between 10 and 11:30 A.M., 30 percent; after 11:30 A.M., 13 percent. When stories were filed in fragments over a period of time, the later fragments presumably reporting later developments, were more often discarded than those received earlier.

There are other non-news factors that influence what the reader will see. Space for news varies from day to day not on the basis of news events but on when American families plan their weekly shopping. Those are the days when department stores, used-car dealers and supermarkets do their maximum advertising. Since quantity of advertising determines quantity of news, there is minimum news space on Saturdays, Mondays, and Tuesdays, and maximum space on Wednesdays, Thursdays and Fridays.

But the maximum news space on maximum advertising days does not help much to increase the quota of late news. Mechanical departments producing a twenty-four-page paper, as they might on a Saturday, reserve their last hour for the few pages, like page one, that are prime news display spaces and receive news until the last minute. When the same staff put out a ninety-six-page paper, as they might on a Thursday, they require the same time for these last late-news pages. So they must work even faster in the early hours of the publishing cycle to process the larger number of total pages. On such a day, the gatekeeper must send out masses of news very early in the editing cycle, to fill up the added pages. Very early stories tend to have no time relevance and often no other kind except that they are available and fill space.

This process is raised to a level of exquisite frustration by the fact that the gatekeeper may be informed in the middle of his day that his available news space has changed.

The Gatekeeper's Dilemma

In all of this, the gatekeeper is haunted by two opposite perils. One is failing to send out enough copy to fill his allotted space. If this happens, there are empty columns and the paper cannot go to press on time, a psychic trauma on a newspaper. It is also a logistic one: fleets of delivery trucks are on minute-by-minute schedules, bundles of papers have to make trains and planes, and networks of newsboys must get their papers on time or else will, on a morning paper, abandon their paper routes for school. An evening paper's trucks will get stalled in rush-hour traffic and the paper will be delivered to the home after 5:30 P.M., by which time most papers assume they have lost the reader to the evening meal and television.

On the other hand, if the gatekeeper sends out too much news, he will get a report each day on how much this has cost the paper. Excess news that has been set in type but not used costs hundreds of dollars and the daily amount of wastage is a figure most managements take pains to circulate to those responsible.

So decisions on what news goes into a daily paper and what stays out are not made in serenity with full knowledge of alternatives. Each story is not judged solely on the basis of its importance compared to all other stories available that day. Instead it is compared to stories already committed to print and to stories not yet seen. The editor must also consider how much time and space remain, and how much money and time it will cost to reverse earlier decisions on the basis of later and better information.

On one suburban evening paper of less than fifty thousand circulation, the news editor arrives at 6 A.M. to find an overnight accumulation of fifty thousand words, most of it regional and na-tional news from three wire-service machines, some of it from the paper's reporters in outlying bureaus, who transmitted it by teletype the night before.

In addition to making decisions on incoming wire stories, this particular news editor makes decisions on local stories handed him by the city editor and the state editor. He also is handed the output of two wirephoto machines that during the day produce ninety-six photographs, from which he selects sixteen. He must commit his photographs much earlier than his texts since mechanical processing of pictures is time consuming. Though the presses are not scheduled to roll until 1 P.M., most photos must be selected by 8 A.M.

In his first hour, in addition to going through the accumulated fifty thousand words, the news editor also makes a rough dummy of page one, drawing in the stories as he predicts them at that moment. His decisions on which stories will go on page one are frequently influenced by whether there are good photographs to accompany them. But photo decisions have to be completed four hours before the last text decisions.

At 8:30 A.M. a secretary hands the news editor mailed press releases which he looks through for five minutes. Then the news editor is offered a local story but after consulting a pad on his desk announces that he already has too many stories for the available space. Shortly afterward the secretary hands him a second batch of mailed press releases, but having just determined that he is running out of available space, the news editor throws away the releases unopened.

At 10 A.M. a new page-one dummy is drawn. At 11:30 it is redrawn and the original story that was going to lead the paper is pushed to the inside. At 11:40 the news editor discovers that he miscalculated on available space and instead of being oversupplied is undersupplied. He quickly sends out earlier stories that were rejected. Twenty minutes later, the city editor shows him page one of the first edition of a paper in a nearby metropolis and the news editor changes his headline to conform with a more interesting emphasis made by the big-city paper. Fifteen minutes after that, a wire service sends a completely new story on the same subject, and he throws out the entire previous story and uses the new one, which requires changing the metal plates for page one which had already been cast. This decision increases the amount of daily type he has ordered but will not use. And it misses the printing deadline slightly, which is not so serious since this is a one-edition paper with a relatively simple distribution system.

Thus, during seven hours, the staff, headed by the gatekeeper, who made almost all the initial decisions, processed about 110,000 words, or the equivalent of a book. And did a number of other demanding tasks at the same time. A book-publishing house normally takes from six months to a year to process a book with the same quantity of information. The content of a newspaper is very different from that of the average book, but the difference in their technology and working styles is striking.

While Customers Sleep

Morning papers which, in the United States, constitute 18 percent of all dailies with 41 percent of all circulation, are less hurried than evening papers. Most public events occur during the day, so a morning paper can make its decisions after most of the business of the nation has been completed and the number of unpredicted new items

falls off. A morning paper's production and distribution are completed while its customers are asleep and are not being informed by radio, television, telephone, and word-of-mouth of all the latest developments. While the most important working hours for editors who produce afternoon papers are from 6 A.M. to noon, those for morning papers are 3 P.M. to midnight. A dramatic event at 11 A.M. must be reported without delay by an afternoon paper whose printing may be only an hour away. A dramatic event at 5 P.M. gives a morning paper three to five hours before printing in which to confirm, add details, provide background and interpretation. Ironically, afternoon papers are the ones whose headline news has been pre-empted by broadcasting and which therefore are under the greatest pressure to provide confirmation, details, background, and interpretation.

On one metropolitan afternoon paper there is a very large gross intake of words and stories, for just the regional and national news, of over 400,000 words and 2,500 different news items, coming from 22 teletype machines, most of which operate 24 hours a day. The paper used 40,000 words in 300 items. This is not counting information coming in for special departments like sports and financial.

From 6 P.M., after the last edition of this large afternoon paper has gone to press, to 1 A.M. there is a skeleton staff reading and processing incoming stories for the next day's paper, sending from two to five stories an hour for typesetting. There is an increase in numbers of stories selected between 1 and 2 A.M., which is after most morning papers have gone to press, thus making post-one-o'clock news usable for afternoon papers, even though these papers will not be delivered to suburban homes until thirteen hours later. There is another peak in numbers of stories sent for processing between 6 and 7 A.M., when the full-time staff begins its day, and another peak between 10 and 11 A.M., when the latest possible news is pushed into the paper.

The initial yes-no decision on the 2,500 stories with 400,000 words is made by three men, one in charge of political national news, one of other national news, and the other of regional news. The latter two simultaneously direct their staffs. But there is a difference in the nature of the handling on the larger paper. Almost every story selected for insertion in this metropolitan paper, once the gatekeeper had taken the usual seconds to make his decision, was then handed to a reporter or rewrite man to read, check, compare with other stories on the same subject, and, usually, to rewrite.

So, while the gatekeepers on the large paper each handled twice the wordage of the gatekeeper on a small paper, the stories they selected were subject to relatively careful and individualistic treatment. Yet they discarded 90 percent of incoming stories and for the most part their decisions on the discards were irreversible.

On the basis of observations during the study, the typical gatekeeper of news makes his decisions with remarkable speed. Discarded stories took from one to two seconds of reading each. The time taken for the initial decision on stories destined to go into the paper was somewhat longer, but not a great deal on the average. On stories selected for use, the gatekeeper usually seemed to scan the entire story, judging from the movement of his eyes but also from the fact that he occasionally caught a typographical error and compulsively corrected it in the latter part of the story.

One very fast gatekeeper took an average of

four seconds to handle (read, decide to use it, and indicate the changes he wanted made) a story of 225 words. Shorter items used would take two seconds, longer ones ten seconds at a maximum. The average for observed gatekeepers was about six seconds per story selected for use.

This is a virtuoso performance of decision making. Judgment is exercised almost instantly without time for reflection or references. Whatever values the gatekeeper brings to these decisions he brings by reflex.

Other Pressures

What is the basis for these reflex decisions on what becomes American public affairs?

It would be naïve to think that only some abstract professional standard determines whether stories will be printed. The editor who assigns a reporter has his personal values involved, and so does the reporter who decides which facts to report in what context; so does the gatekeeper who winnows the finished items destined to be printed, and so does the owner of the journalism corporation who employs them all. These personal values are in shifting equilibrium with professional standards of fairness and proof.

It would not be realistic to think that the gatekeeper is completely insulated from official policy on the paper. In one study of contemporary journalism, the author describes the unstated but pervasive presence of publishers' values in the decisions of working journalists, including the gatekeepers.

Official news policy is usually vague and almost never spelled out to any journalist because of the taboo in the trade against tampering with facts. Newspapers, especially monopoly newspapers, are expected to be objective in the sense that they provide equitable access to the news columns and fair treatment of topics and individuals. Cases in which owners or executives order the suppression of stories or their insertion for "policy" reasons are met with disapproval in the trade.

Nevertheless, policy is exerted in effective ways. Editorial executives control the assignment of stories, which is the most crucial decision in journalism. They decide whether the finished story will be used or not, and if used, with what emphasis and length, and whether or not the reporter's name will appear on it. Rewards and punishments for reporters are almost never explicitly on the basis of adherence to official policy, but on most papers it is clear to the staff that stories of a certain kind receive rewards and in many papers these are stories that please the proprietor. . . .

On the other hand, the reporter has considerable control over the recounting of facts. If he insists on a particular description of a situation, it is unusual for a superior to overrule him on grounds of policy: unless a story can be attacked on grounds of accuracy, significance, or reasoning, even a disapproving superior will feel obligated to print it. There is hesitation to fire a journalist for reportorial nonconformity to a paper's economic or social policy, since this is regarded in the trade as unethical behavior by management; where there is a reporters' union it is forbidden by contract. There is far less hesitation to fire the reporter's superior for failure to conform to a publisher's ideas. In this ambiguity, social rather than direct pressures are the dominant mechanism for encouraging conformity to the political and social policy of the journalistic corporation.

A number of factors inhibit these pressures, though they do not eliminate them. Primary is the almost universal contempt among professional journalists for anyone who deliberately distorts information. . . .

Professionalism is increasing. Reporters and correspondents are better educated and more independent than in the past. The qualities of a good journalist—disciplined observation with an ability to write clearly—are in such demand in other occupations that the competition for the best journalists has enhanced their standing in their own trade and strengthened professionalism within news corporations.

Readers are more sophisticated and better informed than before. The proliferation of alternative sources of information has made the audience more critical and able to compare accounts. Many events are seen directly on television in their original form, or listened to on radio, ending the exclusive power of second-hand printed reports. . . .

So the gatekeeper, though he seems to perform like one, is not an unfeeling machine operating in a social vacuum. His decisions, resulting in the printing of most stories seen by the public, reflect his personal as well as his professional values, and all the surrounding pressures that converge on him. . . .

What's Ahead

The printed news system is like a funnel with five times more material pouring into the top than can come out of the bottom, with a few crucial men controlling the valve that passes one story for every four that is rejected. By far the greatest volume poured into the funnel comes from outside the city, on teletype machines that now produce news at the rate of 45 words a minute. Selecting the few stories that will fit into the paper and be comprehensible to readers is now a process that seems to reach the limits of human speed and judgment. Yet there are replacements for the present teletype machines that in the near future will deliver 1,050 words a minute, still another design that will deliver 2,400 words a minute, and finally one that will transfer a full news report from a central computer into a local newspaper computer at the rate of 86,000 words a minute. These are, respectively, 23 times, 53 times, and 1,900 times faster than the machines that present news to local editors today. Such speeds make clear the obsolescence of even recent methods of converting words into print: 5.6 lines a minute cast in 1932, 14 lines in 1960, 1,800 lines in 1966, 15,000 lines in 1967. The rapid reception of information and its rapid conversion into a printed form presentable to a mass audience will mean that men and procedures now used to produce the daily news will undergo fundamental change and with that will come a change in the nature of the news itself. . . .

The selection process that now has the gatekeeper selecting 100 items out of 500, or, on a large metropolitan paper, 300 items out of 2,500, may in the future force him to select the same number of items from a much larger total. The editing process, already crucial since it is the step that eliminates 80 to 90 percent of all incoming matter from reader consideration, will become even more powerful and demanding. Editors will become increasingly important and their personal values more influential.

How rapidly information is edited and after what degree of comprehensive accumulation will depend on how the manufacturing stages of a newspaper can be accelerated. If they remain as they are today, the increased reception and editing of news will have minimal effect, since the editors will still have to feed the production machine slowly and continuously throughout the day. The greatest delays in printed news are not in the compiling of news but in its conversion to print.

If, however, the manufacturing process is shortened, it will permit full and up-to-date review of the total report of the day before final decisions are made and the results placed massively into the production stages.

If, in addition to that, later home systems permit display of a standard news package in the home, with the consumer able to order additional material, the editing process will change even more. In that case, the 80 or 90 or 99 percent of all stories eliminated by the editor for the standard package can remain in the computer, for callup by consumers. The consumer on his video screen might, for example, see an index of the total available stories, just as the editor did in selecting the standard package, and, like the editor, the consumer will be able to select which stories and how much of any story he wishes to see. . . .

It is likely that the average citizen, like the average scientist, scholar, and professional, will learn to scan his literature by abstracts and indexes, and that news organizations will increasingly offer him such a rapid daily inventory. It is also probable that a standard display of news will continue to be presented, in printed form delivered to the home and, much later, transmitted electronically. But there will probably be available either on continuous special channels or on the basis of orders sent out from the consumer's home console, added depth and breadth of news that will make each citizen his own editor. This will end the finality of the gatekeeper decision, and wisely so since the gathering of news spreads wider and its intensity and detail get deeper as the years pass. But until some way is found to give the citizen greater access to this enlarged reservoir, the decisions of even the wisest gatekeepers will become increasingly difficult.

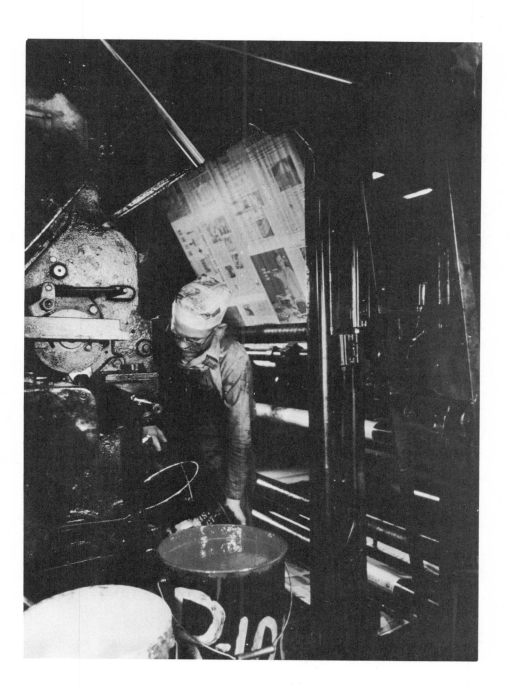

Humor in the Headlines

Dealers Will Hear Car Talk
Friday Noon

Newark (N.J.) News

Men Recommend More Clubs For Wives

New York (N.Y.) Herald Tribune

Many Antiques
at D.A.R. Meeting

Redondo Beach (Calif.) Daily Breeze

Salesman Says He Left 4 Large Rings
in Malden Motel Bathtub

Malden (Mass.) News

10 REVOLTING OFFICERS EXECUTED

Twin Falls (Idaho) Times-News

QUARTER OF A MILLION CHINESE LIVE ON WATER

Schenectady (N.Y.) Gazette

Donald Blank Fulfills
Last Duty to His City, Dies

Memphis (Tenn.) Commercial Appeal

Fine GI's Wife For Sale in Black Market

New York (N.Y.) Post

Portland Rabbi Gives Birth to 20 Bunnies

St. Louis (Mo.) Star-Times

TRAFFIC DEAD RISE SLOWLY

Hobbs (N.M.) News-Sun

Fine Young Man Convicted of Misdemeanor

Portland (Ore.) Daily Reporter

Man Held in Miami After Shooting Bee

Jacksonville (Fla.) Times-Union

COUNTY OFFICIALS TO TALK RUBBISH

Los Angeles (Calif.) Mirror

Autos Killing 110 a Day; Let's Resolve to do Better

Boston (Mass.) Sunday Globe

New Autos May Hit 5 Million

San Francisco (Calif.) Examiner

Town to Drop School Bus When Overpass is Ready

Providence (R.I.) Evening Bulletin

Meat Head Fights Hike in Minimum Pay

Houston (Tex.) Daily Press

Grandmother of Eight Makes Hole in One

Blackfoot (Idaho) News

HERSHEY BARS PROTEST

New York (N.Y.) Civil Liberties

Bone Heads Study Group to Visit Egypt Schools

St. Louis (Mo.) Post-Dispatch

Lawyers to Offer Poor Free Advice

Denver (Colo.) Rocky Mountain News

CALF BORN TO FARMER WITH TWO HEADS

Houston (Tex.) Daily Press

IKE SAYS NIXON CAN'T STAND PAT

Macon (Ga.) News

Admits Shooting Husband From Stand During Trial

Pittsburgh (Pa.) Press

Katherine Wright Ends Long Friendship by Marriage to Kansas Editor

Cincinnati (Ohio) Post

Interpreting the News

What They Say...	What It Means...
...today, a White House spokesman revealed...	...today, a White House spokesman finally revealed what everybody else already knew...
...first reports had indicated...	...first reports were all wrong...
...and after a long investigation...	...a Stoolie finally came through...
...vows to remain on the job...	...everybody wants him off the job...
...a relentless effort will be made to find the killer...	...there's no chance of ever finding the killer...
...has offered no comment...	...is too embarrassed to comment...
...surveillance has been increased...	...they still haven't found anything...
...but terms of the contract have not been disclosed...	...the Rank and File will get the short end again...
...are calling the blaze suspicious...	...looks like the Arsonist got away...
...has introduced a bill into Congress which would effect far-reaching reforms...	...the Congress will defeat a bill which would have effected far-reaching reforms...
...faces a maximum penalty of 20 years in prison...	...will get 6 months, with a suspended sentence...
...who has his eye on the Gubernatorial contest...	...who's been making deals like crazy for months...
...and it is alleged by an unidentified source...	...somebody's trying to get somebody into trouble...
...is leaving his post to devote more time to his family...	...was fired...
...in a surprise statement...	...in a statement he was warned not to make...

A novelist may be defined as a person who,
in order to tell the truth, relates one lie after another.
His writing is what we call fiction.

A journalist, on the other hand, has been defined
as a person who, in order to tell a lie,
relates one truth after the other.
We call this kind of writing nonfiction.

Today we played a big murder, two accidents,
   and a society divorce.
The UN and the new bond issues got secondary play.
We say, "But that is the stuff people are interested in.
That's what sells the paper." But is it right?

A Midwestern Editor

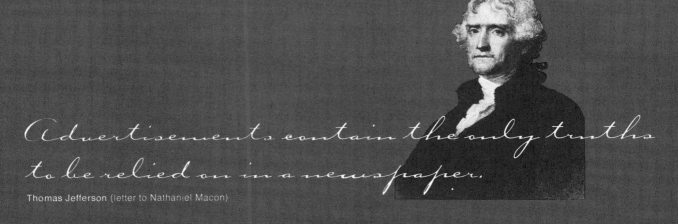

Advertisements contain the only truths
to be relied on in a newspaper.

Thomas Jefferson (letter to Nathaniel Macon)

Journalists and ad men agree that this is
a half-truth but are unable to agree which half
is truthful.

Bergen Evans

ADVERTISING

FUNK'S ∘ CREAM ∘ OF ∘ ROSES

BEATS THE WORLD.

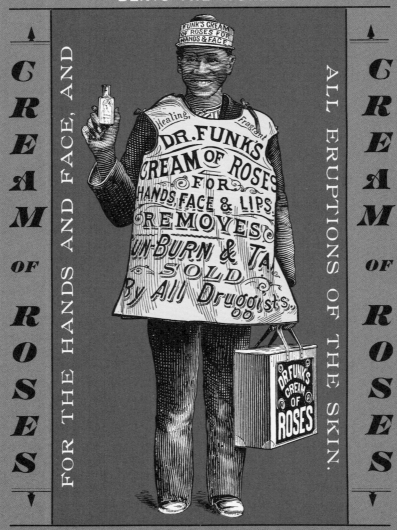

FOR THE HANDS AND FACE, AND

ALL ERUPTIONS OF THE SKIN.

CREAM OF ROSES

CREAM OF ROSES

FOR CHAPPED HANDS, FACE, ETC.

ADVERTISING THROUGH THE MASS MEDIA

MAX BRAITHWAITE

Advertising nourishes the consuming power of men.
It sets up before a man the goal of a better home,
better clothing, better food for himself and his family.
It spurs individual exertion and greater production.
SIR WINSTON CHURCHILL

The advertising man . . . seduces the minds of our children with false and
meretricious values, undermines the editorial freedom of the press, and entices
innocent housewives to spend more and more money on things they need less
and less.
"The Advertising Man," by Jeremy Tunstall,
from *The Listener.*

These two statements are representative of the pros and cons of modern thinking about advertising.

In its simplest form, advertising is a tool used by a seller to convince the public to buy his goods. Prior to the invention of printing, sellers hired people to run through the streets shouting the virtues of their wares; in short, advertising them. In modern times, advertising is the principal support of newspapers and magazines. Thus it has a great deal of influence on information and entertainment found in those media.

With the introduction of radio and television, the quantity and insistence of advertisements greatly increased. It is estimated that, through all media, a modern family is confronted with no less than 1,450 advertisements a day. This constant harangue, continually enhanced by new audio and visual tricks, cannot fail to affect our attitudes, habits, styles, manners, and morals, and hence determines, to a considerable extent, how we live.

Large-scale advertising is planned, produced, and sold by agencies which receive for their services a percentage of the money spent on advertising. These agencies hire the best available organizers, psychologists, artists, and writers to devise better methods of influencing us to buy their sponsors' products.

The Latin phrase, *caveat emptor* meaning "let the buyer beware," is one that might well be applied to modern advertising. In other words, the vendor may use every legal means to sell his goods profitably; the consumer, to protect *his* interests, should apply his knowledge and intelligence in deciding what he will buy.

Over the years, display techniques have improved tremendously. Better photography, lithography, printing, papers, etc. have made it possible to produce beautiful art work, especially on the high-gloss papers of expensive magazines. In some of these magazines, the advertisements are almost as entertaining as the stories, articles, and special features.

Arguments about the value of advertising are rather dreary to listen to. The advocates of advertising (and these are usually people who use or produce advertising) tend to give credit to advertising for almost all of man's economic and social progress since the invention of the steam engine. Its opponents say that all advertising is wasteful and that its full costs are paid by the buyer of the product advertised. Actually neither view is correct—in part because it's impossible to make any general statement that applies to *all* advertising. There are two basic types of advertising, and each of them presents quite different problems to its audience.

PRODUCT DIFFERENTIATION

The first type, which focuses on product differentiation, is familiar to you in advertisements for gasoline, automobiles, cigarettes, lipstick, and many other products. Because these products are essentially the same in quality, no matter who makes them, and they are often sold at identical prices, the task of the advertisement is to convince you that Brand A is somehow better than Brand B. The ad can't convince you that Brand A is cheaper (because it isn't), and it can't convince you that Brand A is made better (either because it isn't or because the explanation is too technical). Hence the ad must dwell on such ideas as that owning Brand A is more pleasurable, or that "nicer people" use Brand A, or that Brand A gives you some vague or unspecified advantages that Brand B doesn't have.

Perfume advertising offers some of the most blatant examples of this sort of irrationality in advertising. If one perfume ad presents a picture of a sexy young man saying, "I can't seem to forget you. . . . Your Wind Song stays on my mind" and the competing brand has a picture of a young girl and the lines, "If deep inside, in that silent place, you want to be loved as quiet things are loved, shouldn't your perfume be 'Je Reviens'," you really don't have much basis for a sensible choice between the two.

If you bear in mind that laboratory tests show that all gasoline brands of the same octane rating perform essentially alike in an automobile engine, and if you then look at the competing gasoline ads, you'll understand the techniques of product differentiation. One brand may promise you "happy motoring"; another offers you "fast starts"; none of them tells you that Brand A *is actually better*—because, of course, it isn't.

Look, also, at ads for various makes of automobiles at the same price level. Here again the words and pictures are devoted not to precise technical information but to giving you a vague good feeling about the car. Actually, one study of car advertising found that the most avid readers of car ads were not the prospective buyers but people who had already bought a car and were now reading the ads for it in order to reassure themselves that they had made a good choice.

Product-differentiation advertising is most vulnerable to the charge that it adds to the cost of the product and does its readers no good. Aside from the fact that you're paying for such ads, you learn nothing from them that will help you make a good choice when you buy. Do you *really* choose your breakfast cereal because it's the "breakfast of champions"? And do you *really* believe that one brand of gasoline gives you "happy motoring"?

You can, of course, argue that such ads are just silly and that nobody pays them much attention. But the fact is that the "breakfast of champions" is substantially more expensive than less advertised cereals and that the gasoline that promises you "happy motoring" costs several cents more per gallon than the unadvertised brand that makes no claims but drives your car just as far. Economists estimate that as much as 20 to 40 per cent of the price of each toothpaste and breakfast cereal goes to pay for the advertisements and radio and television commercials for that make—and they argue that a "disarmament agreement" among competing brands to reduce advertising could lower prices without the loss of sales.

INFORMATIVE ADVERTISING

Our second type of advertising can be much more useful, because it tells you things you want to know

As this excerpt from a Sears, Roebuck catalog indicates, mail-order catalogs offer you clear information that can be helpful in your general shopping.

Sears Riding Helmets with floating cap help reduce impact to protect against head injuries

$13⁸⁵ to $24⁹⁵

(3 thru 5) Constructed to exceed Z90.1 specifications of the American National Standards Institute, Inc. Also exceed standards set by Motorcycle Industry Council, Inc. Patented "Y-D" shaped hold-down harness of vinyl-covered nylon. Vinyl extrusion around edge of helmet for added protection. High-visibility glossy white outer shell is scuff and scratch-resistant . . cleans with damp cloth. Floating cap design disperses force of impact to helmet liner . . acts as a cushion to cut down injury. Snaps let you mount visor or face shield. (*Order face shields below*). D-ring provided to adjust chin cup. Reflector strip kit incl. Adjusts to fit various head sizes.

3 **Our best Riding Helmet.** Full floating cap covers entire liner. Includes snap-on, non-glare blue visor. Front of "Y-D" hold-down harness extra thick for greater comfort. Snap-in cold weather adapter fills in ear openings for winter riding warmth. Fabric-covered headband.
28 A 7504—Shipping weight 2 pounds 12 ounces......$24.95

4 **Moderately-priced Riding Helmet.** Full-floating cap completely covers liner. Snap-on non-glare blue visor included. Vinyl-covered headband.
28 A 7505—Shipping weight 2 pounds 15 ounces......$18.95

Even at this Low, Low Price .... **$13⁸⁵** .... . . a Riding Helmet with partial floating cap

5 Meets all necessary standards cited above . . gives protection *plus* comfort while you ride.
28 A 7534—Shipping weight 3 pounds...............$13.85

about the product: how it's made, what it will do, or how much it costs. To see informative advertising at its best, leaf through a big catalog of Sears, Roebuck or J. C. Penny—two of the country's biggest mail-order houses. You'll note the absence of emotional phrases or other come-ons; instead, the copy describes each item carefully and accurately, even pointing out some of its limitations.

Informative advertising can, of course, be misleading, but, the more specific its information, the less likely it is to mislead. For one thing, such federal agencies as the Federal Trade Commission and the Food and Drug Administration protect you against some forms of downright deception. (For example, no retailer will advertise a ring or a tie tack as "sterling silver" or "14 kt. gold" unless it actually is made of such metal). Of course, these federal agencies don't have enough money or staff to police all ads or to make their rules so strict that all loopholes are plugged. (For example, a pair of earrings made of plastic and sprayed with shiny yellow paint can be advertised as "golden," and this may fool some unsophisticated buyers.) But in general you are far better off with the informational ad (which tells you that the _____

typewriter has automatic tabulation, a 12-inch carriage, and an electric carriage return) than with the product-differentiation type that simply urges you to "Swing into the '70's with a _____ typewriter."

READING THE SALES ADS

Probably the most useful type of informational ad is the one that tells you that a certain product is going to be sold at a certain place at a certain price. Department-store sale ads are of this type. Here the emphasis is not so much on the product (the ad assumes you know something about it) as on the price, which has, presumably, been reduced to an attractive level. But, to find how much of a bargain these ads promise, you need to know something about the special vocabulary they use. Almost every time a sale price is specified, it is compared to some other, higher price, and hence you need to know whether the former, higher price was genuine or was something dreamed up by the person who wrote the ad. Here, for example, are some of the terms that might be used in an ad that offers a hi-fi set on sale for "only $149.95":

This ad contains a mixture of the meaningful and the meaningless. Such phrases as "below original wholesale" or "way below dealer cost" can be safely ignored, because no dealer stays in business by selling merchandise for less then he pays for it. But note that the model numbers of the items are specified; this enables you to shop around for comparable prices elsewhere.

"List price $199.95." This is the retail price "suggested" by the manufacturer, and it may even be printed on the carton, but there's no need to take it seriously because relatively few products actually sell at list price. Phonograph records commonly sell for 25 or 35 percent off list; record players and electric appliances, from 10 to 20 percent off. You should expect to pay list price only (1) if you're buying one of the relatively few "fair traded" (that is, price-fixed) items, which are sold everywhere at identical prices; (2) if you're at the mercy of the only store in town that carries what you're looking for (in which case the price may even be higher than list); or (3) if the store offers a full array of desirable (to you) services—excellent sales help, home delivery, charge accounts, and a liberal return policy. The fact that a price is "below list" doesn't guarantee a bargain. Most prices are below list; the real bargains are *farther below* than the others.

"Regularly $199.95." This means (if the store is to be trusted) that the $149.95 price is temporary and that the hi-fi will go back to $199.95 as soon as the sale is over.

"Originally $199.95." All this means is that *once upon a time* (maybe as long as five years ago) the hi-fi was priced at $199.95. It may not have sold well at that price, or it may have been discontinued (either because it didn't work well or because it worked perfectly but was too expensive to manufacture), or it may have been replaced by a better and possibly cheaper model. But, if you know what you're buying, merchandise thus advertised may be a good bargain.

"Below manufacturer's cost." This looks tempting, but you need to know why the manufacturer is willing to take the loss. Was the item badly designed in the first place? Is it now obsolete because of recent technological changes? If so, are spare parts available, and is it still guaranteed?

"Comparable value $199.95." This means only that the retailer *thinks* the item is worth $199.95, not that it ever sold or will sell at that price. In general, this is the least trustworthy phrase, and it is used least frequently by reputable stores.

Jumbo type and exclamation points don't prove that the merchandise advertised is, in fact, a "spectacular value." To judge an ad of this sort, shop around before taking the advertiser's word.

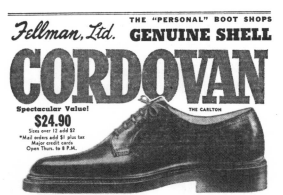

"Was $199.95." This can mean the same as almost any of the above labels. You'll have to ask when and where it was sold at that price, and hope for a reliable answer. *"Special"* is also a meaningless word; *"reduced"* and *"clearance"* can mean as much or as little as the store-owner wants them to mean.

"Special purchase." Approach this one with caution: it may describe a genuine bargain, or it may be a deceptive come-on. Large department stores and chain retailers can make arrangements with a manufacturer to buy a huge quantity of one of his products in return for a very low price, then pass some of the savings on to you. When such a purchase involves the standard product of a reputable manufacturer, you'll be saving money. But some retailers arrange with the manufacturer for a "stripped model" of his standard product—that is, a toaster that carries his brand name but lacks certain features, or a blouse that carries his label but isn't quite as well made as his regular run. Hence, when you see a "special purchase" of cameras or such electric appliances as radios or electric shavers, look for the model number and check with another retailer to see whether the "special" purchase involves the standard current model sold everywhere or a "special" model that is no bargain at the "special" price.

"As is" items are usually priced much below their original price. But you have to examine them carefully when you go shopping. When selling clothing "as is," good stores often pin a piece of paper to any defects to describe them on the tag so that you know why it's "as is"; other stores don't bother. A pulled thread or hole in the front may be conspicuous and impossible to mend; one in the lower back might be mended less noticeably. Garments that are merely soiled can usually be cleaned, but dye or tar stains may not come out. A chipped piece of equipment may work just as well as a perfect one, but be sure to try it out first—the chip may not be the only defect.

"Irregulars" are defined by the Federal Trade Commission as goods that have minor defects, such as an overprinted pattern, knotted threads in the seams, or an oil stain from the sewing machine, that may affect appearance but do not affect durability.

"Seconds," on the other hand, may have the kind of defect that will affect wear—a cut or a dropped yarn in knitted goods, for instance, or an uneven surface in a cooking utensil. Not all seconds have such defects, but they must be examined carefully.

This ad for a springtime clearance may or may not deliver a bargain. Note that you "save $90" only on the $180 items and that the "special selection" may consist largely of items that nobody wanted at their original prices.

Grand Opening. The Sunkist navel is a joy.
It's easier to peel. Easier to segment. And has no seeds.
That's why it's the world's great eating orange.
An easy opening package of what's good for you. Break
into one. And come back to your senses.

Come back to your senses. Sunkist.

How does a deaf, sightless person know when his phone is ringing?

An ordinary household fan—just like this one—tells him.

The fan is turned on by the telephone in the homes of 35 of our deaf, sightless customers. So the instant the phone rings, the fan starts to broadcast a current of air—letting the customer know that his phone is ringing.

It even "looks" for the customer by rotating—to send its silent signal across the entire room.

This simple little idea is one of dozens we've developed at Illinois Bell to help our handicapped customers use their telephones comfortably and conveniently.

They range from highly sophisticated devices like the electronic larynx—which permits people with impaired vocal cords to talk, even over the phone—to special uses of standard equipment. Like Speakerphones® for people who are paralyzed or bedfast. And automatic card dialers with braille writing.

We've designed phones that use flashing light signals to transmit messages for the hard of hearing. And phones that convert sound signals to vibrations for deaf and sightless customers.

And if a customer has a special problem, our engineers will do their best to design or devise an effective solution.

But the only way we can solve the problem is if we know about it. If you know someone who has a physical problem in using the telephone, please phone our Personal Service Specialist at 727-4421. And call collect from the suburbs. We want to help. **Illinois Bell**

We're a lot more than just talk.

He didn't want to spoil his mother's Thanksgiving dinner by being late.

This Thanksgiving, don't drive as though your dinner depended on it.
Drive as though your <u>life</u> depended on it.

Mobil
We want you to live.

4

It's bad enough to be poor. Or sick. Or old.
To be all three is something else.

For most of us, there's always a chance that tomorrow will be a better day. There's always the future.

It's a different story when you're old and penniless. When you've outlived all your friends and loved ones. When what you have today is all you'll ever have.

Think about it. Then do something about it. By giving the United Way you can make somebody's last years a little more comfortable. A little happier.

People are counting on you. The old, the sick, the disturbed, the poor. Help us help. Give the United Way. Please.

If you don't do it, it won't get done.

Feature-by-Feature Advertising

We've all seen ads like the one below . . . where a product is shown and each of its "marvelous" features is described in glowing detail. Sometimes, when a product doesn't really *have* any exciting features, the copy-writer puts his mind to work and makes the rather ordinary features *sound* marvelous. Well, we'd like to show how this technique can be carried to an extreme by making some *really* dull, everyday products sound *very exciting indeed* with the use of—

Telescoping Antenna
for top FM and SW performance.

Outlet for External
Antenna (included) to
help bring in distant
short wave stations.

Convenient Carrying Handle
in matching padded simulated
leather.

Padded Simulated
Leather Case—
**is handsome and
rugged.**

Solid Die Cast
Housing for years of
dependable **service.**

Slide Rule Vernier Tuning
for precise station selection.

8½″ Dynamic Speaker
delivers full, rich
sound on every band.

Short Wave Band
covers 3.8 to 12 MC.

AFC Switch
locks in FM station
for drift-free reception.

Handsome Wood Grain
Control Panel.

116

Introducing The Exciting New
NEET Memo Pad
With These Fabulous Outstanding Features:

EACH PAGE CONTAINS
two complete sides and four precision-trimmed edges!

INGENIOUS RECTANGULAR DESIGN
permits you to fold it anywhere—in half, in thirds, in quarters! Maybe you want it bold and flat for all to see! Maybe you want it folded up tight so no one can see! You decide, and **NEET PADS** obey!

PLAIN WHITE PAPER
just like the type used for writing hit Broadway Shows, the lyrics to Million-Record-Selling Songs, and Life-Saving Prescriptions!

UNIQUE BINDING
holds all the pages and lets you tear them off with a flick of the wrist.

EVERY PAD BACKED
by special cardboard "easel" to give it stability and support—the very same principle used by artists like Norman Rockwell!

500 MATCHING PAGES
to a pad! Use them in order or out of order! They will still match!

MEETS ALL POST OFFICE REGULATIONS.
Pages can be placed in envelopes and mailed First, Second, Third, Air Mail, Special Delivery or any way you desire!

ABSOLUTELY BLANK PAGES.
Allows you to decide for yourself how many lines you want to write on each.

When It Comes to a Culinary Accessory
There Is Nothing In the World Like an

Acme Toothpick

You Can't Beat These Wonderful Features!

*Made from one
of Nature's finest
products: Wood!*

*Natural wood finish,
the same finish found
in furniture costing
thousands of dollars!*

*Lightweight design
and construction
ends inconvenience
of lugging around
"heavy" toothpicks!**

*Neat appearance, lets
you take them anywhere
…from the worst hot
dog stand to the finest
restaurant in the city.*

*Precision-honed tip,
specially designed
to remove all food
particles from your
teeth! You enjoy the
same exact results
as Doctors, Lawyers
and—yes—even Kings!*

*Illustration is 3 times natural size!

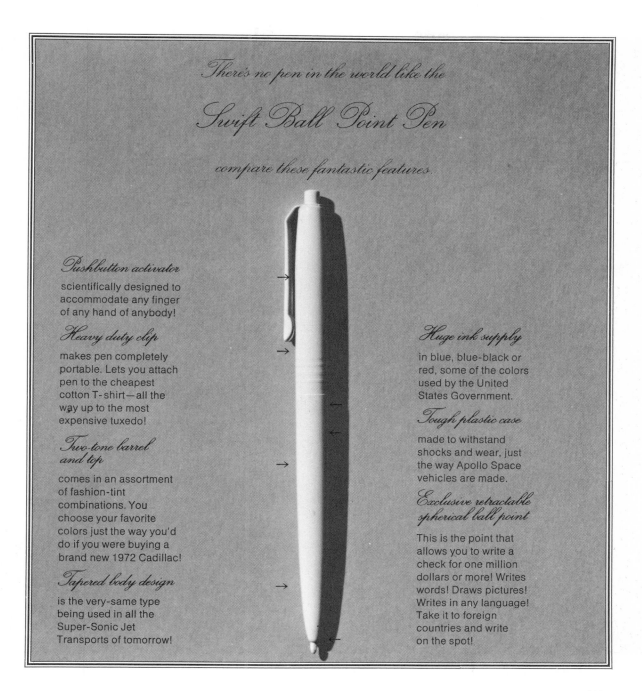

There's no pen in the world like the

Swift Ball Point Pen

compare these fantastic features.

Pushbutton activator

scientifically designed to accommodate any finger of any hand of anybody!

Heavy duty clip

makes pen completely portable. Lets you attach pen to the cheapest cotton T-shirt—all the way up to the most expensive tuxedo!

Two-tone barrel and top

comes in an assortment of fashion-tint combinations. You choose your favorite colors just the way you'd do if you were buying a brand new 1972 Cadillac!

Tapered body design

is the very-same type being used in all the Super-Sonic Jet Transports of tomorrow!

Huge ink supply

in blue, blue-black or red, some of the colors used by the United States Government.

Tough plastic case

made to withstand shocks and wear, just the way Apollo Space vehicles are made.

Exclusive retractable spherical ball point

This is the point that allows you to write a check for one million dollars or more! Writes words! Draws pictures! Writes in any language! Take it to foreign countries and write on the spot!

Can Advertisers Back Up Their Claims?

The FTC asked for facts.

Here's what it got.

A while back the Federal Trade Commission put on as brash a put-up-or-shut-up drive as the Old West ever saw in its prime. To some of the biggest advertisers in the land, the FTC said, in effect: "You say thus and so about your product. Now let's see your proof. What facts back up your claims? Put your cards on the table."

Justifications poured in by the thousands of pages, enabling the FTC staff to compile a report made public by Sen. Frank E. Moss, the Utah Democrat who wants a law to require clear, simple facts to be made available in support of ads that make performance claims.

The report, complete with rebuttal from any company that wanted to give it, criticized many advertising practices. It did note that all but two of the companies questioned had made at least some attempt to support every advertising claim. (Those two admitted that some of their claims were false and said they wouldn't repeat them.) Almost a third of the answers were so technical, though, that the staff said it was not able to evaluate them without expert help.

You can learn a lot from this report about ads you've seen or heard time and again. And you can learn quite a bit that's instructive about advertising claims in general. Consider, for example, some of these details from the report:

Automobiles

The FTC received 1,175 pages of documentation from car manufacturers. The report said that 13 answers lacked any hard facts to support the claims. The data was regarded as incomplete on another 21 claims, including three on gas mileage. The report commented that all the gas mileage claims seemed unrealistic in terms of normal driving conditions. About 43% of the answers, covering 32 claims, simply couldn't be evaluated by laymen.

In some instances there was a sharp difference of opinion between the FTC staff and the manufacturers on whether the material submitted was relevant. The report noted, for example, that Ford's "sole support" for the claim that the Pinto never needs waxing was the assertion that "Ford believes that paints that meet [its] stringent requirements are capable of maintaining an acceptable appearance for an extended number of years." In a rebuttal letter to Sen. Moss, Ford said its complete answer had included a reference to the exposure tests it conducts regularly on paint panels in Florida.

Volkswagen sent a list of 12 engine changes as substantiation for its claim that the 1971 Beetle engine is "longer lasting." The report said that neither endurance tests nor any other data on the changed parts were included. VW later explained that these were engineering conclusions, since insufficient mileage had accumulated to offer lifetime studies.

Chevrolet Chevelle's advertising of "109 advantages" designed to keep it from "becoming old before its time" also was cited. Documentation included such "advantages" as "full line of models," "Body by Fisher," and various safety items that were already required by law.

Electric Shavers

According to the FTC staff, eight of 25 claims were supported by documentation found to be both relevant and reasonably complete. Of the eight, according to the report, seven were supplied by North American Philips. Sunbeam's single submission also was considered sufficient.

North American Philips supported its claim that Norelco's ultra-thin shaving heads make it possible to get a close shave with a 12-page description of a comparative shaving test run on over 100 subjects, plus a laboratory test report indicating that the Norelco shaves below skin level.

Sunbeam documented its claim that the Lady Sunbeam won't nick or cut by furnishing photographs of the shaver's comb and cutter, along with a detailed explanation, test results, and public opinion surveys.

Documentation for 11 other claims was open to question and six more required extra analysis to determine their adequacy.

Sperry Rand, ordered to back its claim that a disposable-blade feature prevents its Remington shavers from wearing out, said the meaning was clear: "Remington's disposable blades will extend the useful life of a Remington shaver whereas a shaver without disposable blades will often be put aside by the user once the blades become dull."

Air-conditioners

The 1,150 pages of fact and explanation sent by the 16 companies questioned were of varying usefulness, according to the report. In two cases companies admitted that their claims were false.

Fedders admitted that a claim of "extra cooling power" for one model was incorrect and said that it would not be used in future advertising. Similarly, National Union Electric admitted that its Emerson 14,000 Btu model was not the "largest" of its kind on the market and said it would not repeat the claim.

Raytheon sent a copy of the installation instructions, apparently believing that would support a claim that the Amana room air-conditioner "takes only minutes to go from carton to cooling."

On claims of quietness, Sears documentation consisted solely of statements about "superb engineering" and a discussion of why a low-speed fan is quieter than a high-speed fan, according to the report. For the same quietness claim Chrysler submitted a graph comparing sound levels of its Tempette model to three competing models. Philco-Ford provided a table of "calculated loudness levels for a variety of air-conditioners."

Television Sets

Every company filed some sort of response on their claims, but in two cases the manufacturers disclaimed responsibility for ads. Magnavox did not send any supporting material for four of ten claims on the grounds that these were created by the advertising departments of the dealer who had placed the ads. These included such statements as "brilliant color tube that assures true flesh tones," "automatic fine tuning gives you a clear color picture" and "the largest, most rectangular screen with TAC (Total Automatic Color)."

Matsushita explained that the ad saying its Panasonic 12-inch portable had "all the features of higher-priced sets" was prepared and placed by the retailer and that none of Matsushita's advertising, literature, and sales promotion material make any reference to such a claim. In contrast, Motorola backed up three claims relating to its Instamatic color tuning feature, although two of these claims were placed by retailers. At the same time, Motorola disclaimed responsibility because it hadn't paid for nor taken part in preparing the ads.

To prove its contention that its 10-inch color model was available at "half the price of many color sets," GE submitted suggested prices for several makes and models, both consoles and portables, in a variety of screen sizes. The report said that while the documentation was adequate, its value to the consumer was questionable since all of the models cited for comparison were larger than the General Electric.

Since the report was made public, advertising industry groups have been urging remedial action to head off passage of a strict law on advertising.

Consumer-oriented groups have been looking into the technical material that the FTC couldn't decipher, just as the staff had originally hoped they would. The FTC has asked a number of manufacturers of other products to substantiate their advertising claims. Sixteen makers of cough and cold remedies, for example, filed reports that said, among other things that the "fever reducer" in Dristan is simply aspirin; that the "children's aspirin" in Congesprin is merely a smaller dose of aspirin; and that the reason Contac ads refer to the summer cold as a "different animal" is that people responding to a survey "perceive a difference between summer and winter colds."

Complaints have been issued against several ads that the FTC has challenged. *(An FTC guide does not have the force of law. The FTC can only issue "cease and desist" orders against violators and go to court to enforce them. Failure to comply, however, can result in a fine and a jail sentence.)*

The manufacturers, of course, must have their say and the issues will be hashed out at length before all the dust settles. Knowing that their claims may be challenged by the government may make advertisers more careful, but as a shopper you can't count on it. The FTC's investigation indicates a number of test questions you can apply to any advertising:

Is the claim so general as to be meaningless, or is it specific?

How does the company support its claims, with facts or vague statements?

Do the advertised features sound gimmicky or truly useful?

Are claims of longevity supported by the warranty?

Whatever the claims—a brighter picture tube, a cleaner and closer shave, better gas mileage —are they convincingly demonstrated to you?

Advertising Portraying or Directed to Women

prepared by a consultive panel of the National Advertising Review Board

The panel's assignment was to examine the basis for complaints about advertising that portrays women or is directed to them. In carrying out its work, the panel drew upon various resources, both inside and outside the advertising industry. It analyzed a broad sampling of current advertising, as well as reviewing in depth the current literature on the subject, both supportive and critical of what is known as "women's liberation."

What the NARB panel found

SCOPE OF THE PROBLEM

Society is undergoing a period of rapid transition. Whether or not you call it a "revolution," the fact is that relationships between the sexes and patterns of social behavior are changing at a swift pace.

Among the pervasive ramifications of this trend, the panel has noted the following random examples:

Educators are rewriting textbooks at every grade level to eliminate traditional sexual stereotypes.

More than twice as many women have had some college training as had it 20 years ago. The number of professional degrees earned by women has also increased significantly.

The U.S. Census Bureau has changed more than 50 job titles to eliminate sex designations. (Office boys are now "office helpers.")

The Conservative Committee on Jewish Law and Standards recently voted to change the practice of centuries by recommending that women be counted as the equals of men in the synagogue.

The leaders of the United Church of Christ were charged by the delegates to the church's Ninth General Synod "to take steps to translate the Bible in a manner sensitive to the experiences of both women and men" and to use "deliberately inclusive language" in hymnals and worship materials.

Women are gaining admittance to more and more clubs and organizations that were formerly exclusively male in membership.

"Ms." as a new form of address for women is gaining acceptance at a steadily increasing pace.

Federal legislation covering fair employment practices as applied to women has been supplemented by a Presidential order prohibiting sex discrimination by federal contractors. Several cases are pending.

In many newspapers classified advertising for employment no longer lists separately the positions available for men and women.

Women are now being accepted in jobs formerly considered as exclusively male, for example, in police and fire departments for patrol duty or as fire fighters. They also have an expanded role in various branches of the military services.

These random statements could be multiplied many times over without including all the important indicators, such as the number of women elected to political office, the amount of back pay awarded to women in cases of employment discrimination, admission of women to professional graduate schools, etc.

In the midst of such far-reaching social change, therefore, it would be surprising if as vital a part of our society as advertising were not affected. It has been. In many instances advertising has already reflected the changing status of women. But it has been attacked for not going far enough, and in some cases for allegedly furthering traditional forms of discrimination against women.

More than ten years ago a Presidential Commission on the Status of Women issued a report, "American Women," which included consideration of the "Portrayal of Women by the Mass Media." Representatives of the communications industry met with members of the commission and, among other matters, discussed how to improve the image of women in the media. One of the consultants spoke of the "uniform, shallow, even grotesque image" of women in television commercials.

SPECIFIC COMPLAINTS

One of the most frequently voiced complaints about advertising is that it portrays women too often just as housewives and mothers—shoppers, cleaners, and family cooks—minimizing their roles in the business and professional world and in community affairs.

Another common complaint is that advertisements often feature women's sexuality to the neglect of their individuality. The charge is that advertising portrays women as "sex objects."

A study reported in the *Journal of Marketing Research* in 1971 found that magazine advertising reflected four stereotypes:

A woman's place is in the home.

Women do not make important decisions or do important things.

Women are dependent on men and need their protection.

Men regard women primarily as sex objects— they are not interested in women as people.

A study of "the image of women in network TV commercials" was reported in the *Journal of Broadcasting* in 1972. On the basis of a content analysis of 986 prime time commercials, the authors concluded that "women are most often seen as decorative (sex objects) or as useful (housewives and mothers), but hardly ever as professionals or working wives." Men were twice as frequently shown in outdoor or business settings as were women. When not in the home, women were shown in a limited number of roles such as secretaries or stewardesses. Only 18 different occupations were shown for women, in contrast to 43 for men. In the sample of television commercials, there were no women lawyers, doctors, business executives, scientists, engineers, athletes, professors, or judges.

PORTRAYAL OF WOMEN AS HOUSEWIVES

One problem about the advertising of household products relates to the matter of cumulative impressions. Any number of individual ads or commercials may be perfectly acceptable when taken one at a time. There is nothing wrong with showing a woman using a household product in the home. An endless procession of commercials on the same theme, however, all showing women using household products in the home, raises very strong implications that women have no other interest except laundry, dishes, waxing floors, and fighting dirt in any form. Seeing a great many such advertisements in succession reinforces the traditional stereotype that a "woman's place is *only* in the home."

It has long been a standard comedy device in the field of entertainment to portray some men and women as stupid. Advertising, in attempting to adapt entertainment techniques, sometimes falls into the trap of attempting to be funny but succeeding only in offending. It is especially true that in the advertising of household products, women too often are portrayed as stupid—too dumb to cope with familiar everyday chores, unless instructed by children, or by a man, or assisted by a supernatural male symbol. Even off-camera voiceover announcements are made by predominantly male voices. In many of the commercials the implication is clear that, if carefully told what to do, a woman can use the product. Ap-

parently, however, it takes a man to manufacture the product or to understand its virtues well enough to explain it.

The advertising of household products often involves psychologically unflattering portrayals of women. In some instances, they are depicted as being obsessed with cleanliness, as being embarrassed or feeling inadequate or guilty because of various forms of household dirt. Other advertisements show women being mean or catty to each other, or being envious or boastful about cooking or cleaning accomplishments in the home.

In summary, the image of the housewife in advertising appears frequently to be not only a circumscribed one, but also a person with a warped sense of values.

PORTRAYAL OF WOMEN AS SEX OBJECTS

The panel believes there is an important difference between portraying a woman as sexy or as having sex appeal, and portraying her as a sex object. Compared to a vibrant, living person with a variety of interests, talents, and normal human characteristics, the woman portrayed as a sex object is like a mannequin, with only the outer shell of a body, however beautiful.

Many women have stated their resentment at the use of the female body as a mere decoration or an attention-getting device in advertising. They feel that such advertising diminishes their own sense of worth, that it ignores and negates other facets of their mind and spirit, and that it belittles women's other attributes and accomplishments. In addition, some women feel that such single-dimensional portrayals of women as sex objects hamper the development of friendships or love between men and women. Also, they deplore the effect on children's values. Many men share these reactions.

PORTRAYAL OF MINORITY WOMEN

The panel found evidence that the same complaints regarding the portrayal of white women in advertising also apply to minority women, including black, oriental, Spanish and others. In this one respect, at least, minority women are treated no worse and no better than white women.

Since blacks constitute the largest minority in this country, they are more frequently portrayed than other minorities in the media of general circulation. In the black-oriented media one sees many of the national campaigns that appear elsewhere, but with blacks taking the place of whites in the illustrations.

What the panel recommends

Recognizing that principles are more enduring than specific cases, the panel has distilled its many months of study into a checklist of questions for advertisers and agency personnel to consider when creating or approving an advertisement.

CHECKLIST: DESTRUCTIVE PORTRAYALS

Am I implying in my promotional campaign that creative, athletic, and mind-enriching toys and games are not for girls as much as for boys? Does my ad, for example, imply that dolls are for girls and chemistry sets are for boys, and that neither could ever become interested in the other category?

Are sexual stereotypes perpetuated in my ad? That is, does it portray women as weak, silly, and overemotional? Or does it picture both sexes as intelligent, physically able, and attractive?

Are the women portrayed in my ad stupid? For example, am I reinforcing the "dumb blonde" cliché? Does my ad portray women who are unable to manage a household without the help of outside experts, particularly male ones?

Does my ad use belittling language? For example, "gal Friday" or "lady professor"? Or "her kitchen" but "his car"? Or "women's chatter" but "men's discussions"?

Does my ad make use of contemptuous phrases? Such as "the weaker sex," "the little woman," "the ball and chain," or "the War Department"?

Do my ads consistently show women waiting on men? Even in occupational situations, for example, are women nurses or secretaries serving coffee, etc., to male bosses or colleagues? And never vice versa?

Is there a gratuitous message in my ads that a woman's most important role in life is a supportive one, to cater to and coddle men and children? Is it a "big deal" when the reverse is shown, that is, very unusual and special—something for which the woman must show gratitude?

Do my ads portray women as more neurotic than men? For example, as ecstatically happy over household cleanliness or deeply depressed because of their failure to achieve near perfection in household tasks?

(A note is needed here, perhaps. It is not the panel's intention to suggest that women never be portrayed in the traditional role of homemaker and mother. We suggest instead that the role of homemaker not be depicted in a grotesque or stereotyped manner, but be treated with the same degree of respect accorded to other important occupations.)

Do my ads feature women who appear to be basically unpleasant? For example, women nagging their husbands or children? Women being condescending to other women? Women being envious or arousing envy? Women playing the "one-upmanship" game (with a sly wink at the camera)?

Do my ads portray women in situations that tend to confirm the view that women are the property of men or are less important than men?

Is there double entendre in my ads? Particularly about sex or women's bodies?

CHECKLIST: NEGATIVE APPEALS

Do my ads try to arouse or play upon stereotyped insecurities? Are women shown as fearful of not being attractive to men or to other women, fearful of not being able to keep their husbands or lovers, fearful of an in-law's disapproval, or, for example, of not being able to cope with a husband's boss coming for dinner?

Does my copy promise unrealistic psychological rewards for using the product? For example, that a perfume can lead to instant romance?

Does my ad blatantly or subtly suggest that the product possesses supernatural powers? If believed literally, is the advertiser unfairly taking advantage of ignorance? Even if understood as hyperbole, does it insult the intelligence of women?

CHECKLIST: CONSTRUCTIVE PORTRAYALS

Are the attitudes and behavior of the women in my ads suitable models for my own daughter to copy? Will I be happy if my own female children grow up to act and react the way the women in my ads act and react?

Do my ads reflect the fact that girls may aspire to careers in business and the professions? Do they show, for example, female doctors and female executives? Some women with both male and female assistants?

Do my ads portray women and men (and children) sharing in the chores of family living? For example, grocery shopping, doing laundry, cooking (not just outdoor barbecueing), washing dishes, cleaning house, taking care of children, mowing the lawn, and other house and yard work?

Do the women in my ads make decisions (or help make them) about the purchase of high-priced items and major family investments? Do they take an informed interest, for example, in insurance and financial matters?

Do my ads portray women actually driving cars and showing an intelligent interest in mechanical features, not just in the color and upholstery?

Are two-income families portrayed in my ads? For example, husband and wife leaving home or returning from work together?

Are the women in my ads doing creative or exciting things? Older women, too? In social and occupational environments? For example, making a speech, in a laboratory, or approving an ad?

CHECKLIST: POSITIVE APPEALS

Is the product presented as a means for a woman to enhance her own self-esteem, to be a beautiful human being, to realize her full potential?

Does my advertisement promise women realistic rewards for using the product? Does it assume intelligence on the part of women?

The panel hopes that its report will encourage advertisers and advertising agencies to look at their work with new eyes, to think of their audience in terms of real people and not bloodless statistics, and to put themselves in the place of those depicted and appealed to—both men and women—and then ask themselves, "How would I like to be depicted in this way?"

NOTHING PERSONAL

James Baldwin

I used to distract myself, some mornings before I got out of bed,
by pressing the television remote control gadget
from one channel to another.

This may be the only way to watch TV: I certainly saw
some remarkable sights.

Blondes and brunettes and, possibly, redheads—my screen was colorless—
washing their hair, relentlessly smiling,
teeth gleaming like the grillwork of automobiles,
breasts firmly, chillingly encased—
            packaged, as it were—
and brilliantly uplifted, forever, all sagging corrected, forever,
all middle age bulge—Middle Age Bulge!—defeated,
eyes as sensuous and mysterious as jelly beans,
lips covered with cellophane,
hair sprayed to the consistency of aluminum,
girdles forbidden to slide up,
stockings defeated in their subversive tendencies to slide down,
to turn crooked,
            to snag,
                    to run,
                        to tear,
hands prevented from aging by incredibly soft detergents,
fingernails forbidden to break by superbly smooth enamels,
teeth forbidden to decay by mysterious chemical formulas,
all conceivable body odor, under no matter what contingency,

prevented for twenty-four hours of every day,
      forever and forever and forever,
children's bones knit strong by the foresight of vast bakeries,
tobacco robbed of any harmful effects by the addition of mint,
      the removal of nicotine, the presence of filters and
      the length of the cigarette,
tires which cannot betray you,
automobiles which will make you feel proud,
doors which cannot slam on those precious fingers or fingernails,
diagrams illustrating—proving—how swiftly impertinent pain
      can be driven away,
square-jawed youngsters dancing, other square-jawed youngsters,
armed with guitars, or backed by bands, howling;
all of this—and so much more!—
punctuated by the roar of great automobiles, overtaking gangsters,
the spatter of tommy-guns mowing them down,
the rise of the organ as the Heroine braces herself to Tell All,
the moving smile of the housewife who has just won
      a fortune in metal and crockery;

news—news? from where?—
dropping into this sea with the alertness and irrelevancy of pebbles,

sex of an appalling coyness,
cigarette being extended by the virile male toward
      the aluminum and cellophane girl.
They happily blow smoke into each other's face,
      jelly beans, brilliant with desire,
                  grillwork gleaming;

Perhaps—poor, betrayed exiles—they are trying to
discover if, behind all that grillwork, all those barriers,
either of them has a tongue.

MOVIES

THE CAMERA AND THE AUDIENCE

GILBERT SELDES

am convinced that the "illusion of reality" or the "illusion of movement" is only a secondary element, although it is the most striking one, in creating the total movie effect. Several other things affect the average movie-goer more. The first is that in the movies the camera not only sees for the audience, it selects what is to be seen and, in a way, pays attention for the audience. The most striking example is the closeup by which the audience is prevented from thinking about anything except the object shown, but this is only a particular instance of the general effect. When the camera swings from the right side of a room to the left, it is doing what the audience in a theater would do when an actor suddenly crossed the stage or another came in through the door.

But this is only a beginning. The camera naturally corresponds to the way we look *at* or look *for* things, by performing the physical movement for us. It corresponds also to our *interest.* We come into a room in which a party is going on; we aren't sure whether we know many people there; we don't know whether the lover with whom we had a quarrel last night has arrived—and if so, whether the quarrel has been forgotten; actually all our doubts are resolved before we have moved two steps into the room and with only the smallest movements, left to right, of our eyes. But the camera does what the mind and the heart do, as well as what the eyes do: it moves rapidly over the groups of people, it picks out the one or two whom we have known before, it searches for the loved one, it lingers on the expression that tells us whether we are forgiven.

The eye can see across a room, but the mind and the heart need more than the eye can give: intensity and concentration. It is the *mind,* not the eye, that creates long shots and medium shots and close-ups; and the well-handled camera satisfies us by being true to our thoughts and, when it acts for the heart, to our desires.

The great Russian director Serge Eisenstein has provided a perfect example of the opposite use of the camera—to prevent us from seeing too much. Imagine, he says, that we see a woman, her face contorted with terror. The next shot can make us clench our hands with empathic fright or it can make us laugh, for the next shot can be a snarling lion about to leap or a little mouse scurrying away. And the effect would not be at all the same if we had seen woman plus mouse (or lion) together in the first place because we would have had no curiosity as to the cause of her emotion and no suspense.

As long as the camera acts in these ways for us, we have the feeling, as we watch the screen, that we aren't missing anything; a good director, in addition, makes us want to see something in a particular way—close to, the middle distance, far away—and gratifies this desire just in time; so we get in double measure the sense of satisfaction. *And the way the movies tell their stories satisfies us as much as the stories they tell.* These stories may be myths, they may correspond to our most infantile desires, they may be false to the realities of existence, and they may satisfy us because the movies themselves have made us incapable of asking for anything else—all these things *may* be; the certainty is that the way the movies are told is a separate gratification, as legitimate in its essence as that of any other art.

The art closest to the movies (and by extension to television) is music because in each the element of time is so significant. In each the full effect of what we hear or see *at this moment* depends on what has gone before and will in turn produce a further effect on what is to come. In its simplest form, the note we hear is part of a sequence of notes which create the melody, as the woman's face we see at the window connects with the detective we have just seen looking for this woman and with the other man who will presently draw down the blind; and the length of time we see each of these shots and their grouping together create the rhythm of the picture, corresponding to the duration of and accent on the notes in music which create their time signature.

The annihilation of ordinary time is one of the most extraordinary effects the movies can produce. Parallel to the invention of perspective in painting, the invention of cutting in the movies is a landmark in the history of art. For cutting is the essential element in creating a second time-span for the spectator: he lives in his own sense of duration, knowing that sixty minutes and no less make an hour, and at the same time he lives by the durations of the movie, in which it may take half an hour to show the events of ten minutes or a lifetime may be condensed into three hours. We have all seen the way this is done, and, as a simple matter of courtesy, the example chosen should be put together from the works of David Wark Griffith, who was the master of this technique and who combined it with his love of the last-minute rescue in truly classic terms.

You begin with the grizzled pioneer or veteran, alone in his cabin with the child he has rescued; around the cabin the Indians are circling; you go back to the interior of the cabin and our hero feeding the child, and the next time you see the Indians, they are closer. From a hill a scout observes the event and sets out for Fort Dodge. The next time we go into the interior of the cabin, nothing much happens, but the following shot may show us the scout forty miles advanced on his journey; then the Indians coming closer; then the cavalry troop starting. The approach of the Indians to the cabin is mercilessly slowed up and the coming of the cavalry enormously accelerated—but we should not be able to accept either one without the right tempo of cutting.

As the climax approaches, the cutter has three elements at his disposal: the cabin, the Indians, the cavalry; and he can show them in irregular order, turning the screw as tight as he likes by showing us cabin-Indians and again cabin-Indians before he cuts to cavalry. As long as he keeps the situation clearly before us, as long as we are afraid that the cavalry will not arrive in time, there is no limit to the combinations he can use. (Cabin-cavalry-cabin is the only one that destroys the situation.) The cutter controls also and varies the duration of each of the three elements on the screen, and the cameraman has given him one further variation, for he has caught the cavalry or the Indians head-on or from strange angles and the terrain through which the cavalry passes has given him gorges and slopes and fordings and notches to exploit. Still another effect is produced by the solid silent cube of the cabin, the circular movement of the Indians, and the diagonal of the cavalry. So, as he plays a trick with time, the cutter is also using space and form, and a kind of architectural inner structure in the movie begins to make itself felt.

In this handling of parallel action Griffith was breaking out of one literary tradition and into another. He said that he was in debt to Dickens for the idea of the flashback, but he did not seem to know that when he sent his Indians and cavalry into action he was actually suppressing Dicken's favorite device. When Martin Chuzzlewit and Mark Tapley have been launched into the wilds of New York, we leave them there; "Meanwhile," says Dickens, in effect, "what was happening in London?'' There is no ''meanwhile'' in the movies; we live in London and in New York at the same time; and in one way this is close to the choppy effect of certain Elizabethan plays where in Act One we may watch three or four scenes of plots and subplots, with different and unrelated characters, and have no idea of their connection, so that the scenes may all be taking place at the same time. With Shakespeare we begin to get a more orderly presentation, we get the connections more clearly. In the movies the bridges between events are evident, we know that scene five is the dance to which all the characters in scene two have been invited or that scene nine is a hallucination in the mind of one person whom we met in scene eight. That is how future and past are identified for us. But when we need to see everything that is happening in the movies' ''now,'' events interpenetrate and we see ''now'' simultaneously in three different places. (I use the quotation marks because the movies' present tense is not that of radio and television, as I shall explain.)

The flashback is an awkward device for the movies, especially when it becomes like the Greek messenger reporting offstage events—but the events are onstage. It is the man telling how he landed the big fish yesterday while we see him landing the fish, apparently today. It has its uses, to be sure. One of the best flashbacks in history (which I have never seen on film) is the story of the Crucifixion as told by Pontius Pilate in Anatole France's story, ''The Procurator of Judea''—for the irony to come through, we must hear the report of the event twenty years after it happened. But in general the instinct of the great directors has made them limit the flashback to the dream, to maniacal ravings, to confessions (as brilliantly done in *Double Indemnity*) and other such exceptional frameworks—and without the narrator talking to us.

One reason for this is that the flashback imposes one past on another. The movie's present tense is not quite the present. It lies somewhere between the past of fiction and the immediate present of live broadcasting. The novel says: ''He walked'' and television says: ''Look I am walking.'' Perhaps the movies say: ''He was walking.'' In the novel you can even say: ''She had been gone six hours before he had noticed it'' and it is awkward to use the present tense except as a stunt; whereas in radio and television it is almost impossible to throw anything into the past.

One source of the feeling of presentness lies, I suspect, in the way we receive broadcasts in sound and sight; they present themselves, so to speak, before us. The movie is something we know was made some time ago, and this affects our time-relation to it in the opposite way. And it is not merely the time; the place counts, too. We go out to a movie house, finding not the theater, but only its shadow; we get a sense that what we see is something recalled, and if the recollection is clear and emotionally strong, we have great movies; whereas when we see something on television, coming to us at home, it isn't recalled at all, it never happened before this moment. And if this happening is feeble and unworthy, the very sense of actuality damns the program, making it an embarrassment precisely because it is so real.

So we can accept the commonplace that the movies satisfy subconscious longings and repeat racial myths. But we must add the satisfactions that come from the essentials of the movie art. The way the camera sees for us, the way time is related to our desires and fears, the way past and present are interstructured all bring the movie close to our instinctive, not our intellectual, life.

The moment sound arrived, the freedom of the cutter-director was limited by the necessities of the writer. A totally new art of the movies came into being.

It was a far more intricate art because it had to reconcile the flowing images of the silent picture with the broken sequences of dialogue; it had to use picture and cutting to address the subconscious and at the same time let speech address itself to the mind. That mistakes were made in the beginning is not remarkable; the miracle is that a satisfactory art of the sound picture was developed—and the irony of cinematic fate is that this art, in turn, had to be sacrificed to the demands of wide-screen pictures.

The physical essentials of the motion picture from the beginning have been these:

A series of photographs so taken and so projected as to give the illusion of motion;

the ability to control the attention of the spectator by showing as much or as little of any given scene as suits the purpose;

a variety of ways to go from one scene to another (the fade, the dissolve, the direct cut are the familiar ones);

control of the time-sense by breaking any action into many parts, showing the audience some of it, skipping other portions;

creation of various feelings of movement by riding the camera or panning;

creation of a sense of beat or rhythm by the system of cutting.

The first consequence of the big picture is that the camera cannot keep its secrets so well—it is hard to isolate a single element when the view is so wide. (It isn't, incidentally, so high—and if a woman's face betrays terror, the camera can pan down or up to find Eisenstein's mouse or lion—more convincingly than it can move to either side, where, by the logic of the screen, we should see everything.)

The closeup itself can now be used exclusively for dramatic purposes—to concentrate our attention on a single object and prevent us from thinking of anything else. In the past it has been used for identification: to bring us so close to an individual that we could see whether the smile on his face was genial or malicious. This is using the camera for the human eye; when the camera is used for the brain, to concentrate on the one person we want to see at this moment, the closeup must eliminate everyone and everything else. The wide screen is not happiest with one huge head-and-shoulders in the center and a blur of color on both sides. It is a little better when we see one person far to the right or left side facing the opposite end of the screen; the audience, which has accepted a hundred conventions in movie-making and thinks nothing of a man walking with no feet visible, will not balk at simple and sensible devices such as letting the screen be dark at one end with the color gradually coming in full at the point of closeup. The dramatic purpose will be served as long as the eye is not distracted.

The success of costume pictures and others in which large groups of people dominated much of the action was perfectly natural and seems to have established the idea that the wide screen requires long sequences of uninterrupted action, eliminating cuts for closeups and reducing even the number of changes of angle. Dr. E. H. Land, inventor of the Polaroid camera, spoke of the screen as "a flexible, readily changeable version of the living stage," and the experience of many directors of dramatic pictures shows a decided preference for scenes that last much longer, without cutting, than we have been accustomed to. For one thing, there is ample room for movement, and actors walk toward and away from the camera, providing closeups naturally—arriving at the correct spot as they say the significant words, and then retreating. This has an effect totally different from that of the camera riding in to get a closer look at a character, for in the second case we, the audience, go in with the camera, we have a curiosity to be satisfied or some doubts to be resolved and we get the feeling of action when the camera carries us to where our interest lies. And the natural change of size, however smoothly handled, has the defect of its virtue—it cannot be so sudden or dramatic as the mechanical cut.

As long as we follow a scene without cuts, time on the screen is the same as our time—but if we insert another scene lasting ten seconds, we can pretend that five minutes have elapsed by the time we return to the first. A distinct tendency to cut for the sake of cutting, to give the spectator something different to look at every fifteen seconds, was becoming noticeable in Hollywood productions just before the new devices (of the wide screen) came in, and the slowing up of the tempo of cutting for the wider screen is a good corrective. But I doubt whether the movies will for long abandon the traditional cutting system. The manipulation of time and the creation of a flow and rhythm in the movies both are based on this system, and so is some of the pure excitement of the eye. For the most part, these things are absorbed without effort, reaching us below the threshold of our consciousness; while our minds follow the spoken word and our eyes the physical movement of people on the screen, the beat of the picture touches our pulse and we respond to it.

The story that is told may be utterly matter-of-fact; the illusion of movement is now so familiar that it is like any other accepted convention. But wherever the movie touches time, it is as mysterious and primordial as the beating of the heart. Absorbed in new techniques, directors may neglect essentials as they did a generation ago when they immobilized the camera to favor the microphone; but, as they recovered mobility then, so I am confident that they will recover the art of using and manipulating time in the substructure of their pictures.

Fortunately for us and for themselves, the producers of entertainment pay little attention to their own theories. Early radio technicians thought they had in the microphone an instrument for *secret* communication, but they developed broadcasting; and, though all Hollywood will no doubt continue to pride itself on the *realism* of the screen, all Hollywood will probably produce works of the imagination filled with illusion. The value of good principles in these matters is only that they eliminate errors; a producer who knows a great deal about the way people see things and the psychological effect on them of certain shapes and colors and tricks of perspective will not have to make a half-dozen false starts. But the false starts have their value too, exposing error at times and at others exposing the limitations of a theory too rigid for daily use.

The new devices in the movies will ultimately be put into the service of the imagination as well as of reality; in Kipling's words, the wildest dreams of Kew and the (newsreel) facts of Khatmandu will both appear. If a producer wants to think out his problems in advance, the histories of art can be of the greatest help to him.

The great Hollywood empire that ruled American tastes for more than half a century lies in dust, its tyrannical moguls dead or deposed, its back lots empty, its sound stages still, its ranks diminished and in disarray. But out of the ruins of the city of dreams a new film industry is rising.

Today's movies are being shaped by a nexus of forces that no one clearly understands. But certainly among the most powerful of these is the gradual emergence of a new audience, demonstrably younger (62 percent of today's moviegoers are between 12 and 30), better educated, more selective and, most important of all, drastically smaller than the mass audience that supported the old Hollywood system. Over the past decade, it is the needs, tastes, and temperament of this new audience that have given birth to a new kind of American movie.

Inevitably, there are those who see all new movies as signs of a golden age and those who see them, with their themes of dissent and alienation, their anything-goes sexuality, as more false idols of a decadent time. The truth is more complicated and more important. The new film focuses not on some back-lot fantasy landscape, but on Times Square and Queens Boulevard, on the basements, bowling alleys, and backyards of Middle America, on American subcultures like the motorcycle-racing circuit and the world of the oil rigger, the urban underworld, and the violence of the American streets.

These films feature men whose ordinary faces would have condemned them to the secondary status of character actors only a decade ago—like the frail, baldish Jack Nicholson and the unglamorous Dustin Hoffman—and have enlisted the considerable talents of new actresses whose unconventional good looks are as offbeat as the roles they play. The life-styles and attitudes of these new heroes and heroines reflect the dissident outlook of the younger directors, who themselves question the prevailing values of American life. A personal cinema is being born, and in its films can be read the search for a better way of life.

The first flickerings of this new itinerant industry were seen in such successes as Dennis Hopper's *Easy Rider* and Robert Rafelson's *Five Easy Pieces*, in *M*A*S*H* and *Joe* and *Diary of a Mad Housewife*, in *Little Fauss and Big Halsy*. But these were just the harbingers of a whole new wave of American films, conceived and developed by screenwriters and directors, not producers and studio chiefs, and focused in a personal way on American traditions and values.

From the 1920s until after the Second World War, Hollywood was a closed shop. Under the autocratic leadership of men like Harry Cohn at Columbia, Louis B. Mayer at MGM, and Jack Warner at Warner Brothers, Hollywood monopolized the movie industry, making virtually every American film on its own back lots. It held in thrall an American public that cheerfully spent 80 cents of every spectator-amusement dollar at the movies. And, to satisfy this massive consumption, the major companies devised an assembly-line studio system that could turn out a film a week on the premises.

Independent production was all but impossible. The banks abetted the Hollywood hegemony by lending money almost exclusively to the big studios. And, even if a producer could find the funds and facilities to make his own movie, where was he to show it since the studios owned or controlled most of the movie houses? But already, by the late 1940s, the autocracy was cracking. The star players rebelled, and the contract system collapsed. In 1950, the Supreme Court ruled that the studios restrained trade by owning chains of movie theaters. And then came television. The old audience and the sure-fire moneymaker vanished forever.

After a period of panic and sharply declining revenues through the 1950s, the studios met the challenge by turning out the kind of wide-screen, multimillion-dollar spectaculars that television couldn't rival. In the mid-'60 s *The Sound of Music,* which earned a record $72 million, salvaged Fox— and nearly ruined the industry by fathering a series of disasters aimed at imitating its success: *Dr. Dolittle, Star!, Goodbye, Mr. Chips.* "We all spent too much money," conceded Richard Zanuck, "and we're just now coming out from under these enormous inventories."

At the same time, the success of Federico Fellini's *La Dolce Vita* attested to the presence of a large and educated audience eager for films with something to say. Frank and Eleanor Perry's low-budget success, *David and Lisa,* in 1962 demonstrated that America didn't have to rely on foreign films to bring in these people. "Some filmmakers realized that there was and still is a large audience whose interests had been left untapped," says screenwriter Buck Henry. "As the mass audience moved toward TV, an effort was made to accommodate these special tastes."

One such effort, *The Graduate,* rewrote the moviemaking rules. "Every studio turned it down," recalls Henry who wrote the screenplay. "They thought you had to have a movie star and they didn't think Anne Bancroft qualified. They thought you needed a young star to play Benjamin and no such animal existed. And they were suspicious of making a movie from a minor novel. But, of course,

when the picture succeeded, all that thinking changed. *The Graduate* made possible motion pictures in which the theme is the star and the star is the director."

Suddenly, a whole new set of faces appeared in leading roles: Dustin Hoffman, Jack Nicholson, Richard Benjamin, Alan Arkin, Donald Sutherland, Jon Voight, Elliott Gould, Dennis Hopper, Stacy Keach, Frank Langella and Gene Wilder. "Ten years ago, they wanted the kind of face that only a few hundred people in the world possess—the Hollywood face," says Wilder. "They didn't want people who looked like the people in the audience. Now they realize they can make money by letting the audience see actors with whom they can identify." Or, as Richard Zanuck put it: "We're hiring the uglies."

The continued success of independent low-budget films like *Bonnie and Clyde, Rachel, Rachel, Goodbye, Columbus,* and the profitable bike and bikini operation run by American International Pictures foreshadowed another watershed film—*Easy Rider.* With its low risk (it cost $300,000 to make) and its high profits, *Easy Rider* seemed to offer the kind of sure-fire formula the industry had been searching for since the first days of television. But, as the prototype for an explosion of "youth" movies with their instant anti-Establishment stance, it raised the question of quality in an emphatic way.

Many filmmakers have swung away from making movies that rely upon either the youth market or topicality for their success. After the runaway success of *Easy Rider,* the studios had started operating on the slogan, "Make it for under $1 million." But with the success of *Patton,* which cost $12.5 million, and the $10.5 million *Airport,* the industry returned to a state of confusion. "There is definitely a place for big films today," asserted Stanley

Schneider, president of Columbia Pictures, which shot *Nicholas and Alexandra* for a scheduled $8 million. "But when I say 'big,' I don't mean the $15 to $20 million film. We can't afford to risk a company's life on a film that big."

Hollywood these days is dancing in the light of a full moon. Once again, instant jungles and châteaux and schooners and Broadways are materializing on studio back lots all over that amorphous fairyland. Smog or no smog, the creative air is thick with old-fashioned, picture-book stories—many of them concerned lately with earthquakes and other assorted disasters—waiting to be blown up into two hours of all-enveloping dreams. After a chaotic, dispirited time of trying to find their place in a chaotic, dispirited world, American movies are coming back home—to Hollywood. No longer do film crews feel compelled to flee the studio compounds in search of a "new realism" in Texas small towns and New York ghettos; now 50 percent of all shooting is done on the well-trampled sound stages and back lots.

No matter that the lion's share of studio production is still devoted to television. Instead of cowering before the upstart as it did a few years ago, the movie industry is flexing the one muscle that television can never match: sheer, larger-than-life showmanship, whether it be the crumbling of a colossal office building for *Towering Inferno,* the reproduction of Hollywood Boulevard as it was in the 1930s for *The Day of the Locust,* the staging of twenty song-and-dance numbers for Peter Bogdanovich's musical, *At Long Last Love,* or the three-hour sweep of Francis Ford Coppola's sequel, *The Godfather Part II.*

Thanks largely to the outlandish success of a few films like *The Godfather, The Exorcist, The Sting,* and *Chinatown,* the movies are reveling in their most lucrative period in several decades. According to *Daily Variety,* the box-office take in 1974 in the United States alone came to $1.6 billion, the highest since the peak earnings of $1.7 billion in 1946. The public's appetite for the Big Picture has never been more keen.

THE GODFATHER

And for the dreammakers themselves, the stakes have never been higher. With one big commercial payoff to his credit, the once-lowly screenwriter can now command fees well into six figures for "original" stories that may well bear no resemblance to their originality by the time they hit the screen. The price tag for the services of golden-boy directors like Coppola, Bogdanovich, and William Friedkin (*The Exorcist*) is now anywhere from $500,000 to a cool million. For the services of one of the bona fide superstars—Streisand, McQueen, Eastwood, or Redford—well, $2 million isn't too much to pay. On all levels, the old star system is back with a vengence.

Big set. Big stories. Big directors. Big stars. Big money. It is all very heady in the fairyland right now —like a dream. And as in all dreams, the situation is riddled with paradox. "In anxious times, people go to movies to escape their anxieties," says Jack Valenti, president of the Motion Picture Association of America, adding hastily: "There's nothing wrong with escapism art." The less obvious paradox exists in the fairyland itself. Why does everyone in this booming industry seem scared to death?

The reason is simple: the cost of making and distributing what is felt to be potentially successful movies has become prohibitive to all but the major studios—Paramount, Universal, Warner Brothers, Columbia, and Twentieth Century-Fox—and United Artists, which has no production facilities but finances and distributes films by independent producers. "The base price for a union film today," says John Calley, president of the hugely successful Warner Brothers, "is around $800,000. That's just for the paper clips." And the danger of not getting it back is enormous. "In today's cost structure," says Eric Heskow, president of United Artists, "a picture must gross two or three times what it cost to make in order to break even."

To minimize that risk, the major studios are not only sharing production facilities but beginning to form financial alliances—Fox and Warners, for example, teamed up to bankroll the $14 million *Towering Inferno*. The movie companies are also trying to consolidate their strength by edging back to the old contract system of corraling talent: Warners has signed up the dynamic independent producer David Picker (*Lenny*) for several important projects over the next three years, and United Artists has just made a multi-picture deal with Hal Ashby, the hot young director of *The Last Detail* and *Shampoo*.

But the driving concern is with what the audience will go to see. The conventional wisdom is best expressed by Paramount's Bob Evans: "The habit of going to *the movies* is over. But the desire to see *a* movie is bigger than ever. I would rather put more money into fewer films than less on a lot of them. If you're making just another picture, forget it. You can't even get your advertising costs back. But if you have one or two big captivating entertainments a year, it's oil rush time."

TOWERING INFERNO

Weekly theater attendance reached a peak, possibly as high as 90 million, in 1947, when television was just out of the womb. By 1971 nearly every home in America had at least one TV set and theater attendance had plunged to an estimated 18 million a week. In the past year it has climbed back to around 21 million.

And what are people watching on the tube? Movies. They have become the most popular entertainment on television, accounting for more than half of all prime-time network programming and up to 80 percent of the airtime on nonaffiliated stations. Universal Studios turned out more than eighty full-length movies in 1973, breaking the industry record set by Paramount back in 1927. Less than a third of these films went to theaters; the rest were features for TV or feature-length shows like "Columbo."

What television provides is a substantial and reasonably steady income for the studios. For spectacular profit, though, the high-risk theatrical market still has its allure. Paramount's profit on *The Godfather,* for example, already exceeds its investment by more than 1,000 percent. So, when a studio acquires a sensational script, chances are that it will gamble on theatrical release rather than trying to make a safe sale to television.

Studios no longer need acres and acres of production space. Columbia and Warner Brothers recently merged their studio facilities, but both companies have increased their output of films. Paramount's lot is devoid of feature filming right now, yet production is at a high rate. "The whole world's a sound stage today," Al Ruddy (producer of *The Godfather*) points out. With the new lightweight, portable equipment, and compact filming vehicles, such as Cinemobiles, it's cheaper to shoot on location—and you get a much more authentic look.

The newer independent production companies maintain no studio facilities of their own; they simply find locations or rent studio space as their needs dictate. The number of independents is growing rapidly. Although major studios put up the money for a great many of these productions, there are some surprising new sources of capital available to filmmakers. Mattel Toys and Quaker Oats have entered the movie business; so has the *Reader's Digest,* which is producing musical versions of *Tom Sawyer* and *Huckleberry Finn. Playboy* now has an active feature-film division.

The Fabergé cosmetics empire owns one of these new filmmaking subsidiaries, Brut Productions. Its Hollywood operations are run by Marty Rackin, who maintains that the new companies have chosen an opportune moment to get into the movie business.

Rackin speaks with boundless enthusiasm about the great days to come: "There are fantastic new markets for films—cable TV, subscription programs, cassettes," he notes. The new markets he talks about constitute the biggest uncertainty in Hollywood's future. A few years ago the mere mention of pay TV was enough to cause panic in the industry; since then, most of the major studios have started divisions to chase the pay-TV market.

Already in some hotels and hospitals you can pay to see new movies on cassettes or through closed-circuit TV systems. The biggest pay-TV market for movies, however, will be found in private homes and apartment buildings. Seven million Americans now subscribe to cable TV, and the figure is expected to rise to ten million by the end of next year. Some cable systems have a potential load capacity of 500 channels and permit the viewer to transmit as well as receive. The viewer may subscribe to a dial-a-movie system that gives him access to a film library containing thousands of titles. He will pick out the movie he wants, and even choose the time he will see it.

Pay TV still has some powerful enemies, including the theater owners, who fear any advance in home entertainment, and the three big TV networks, which resist any effort to diversify the sources of entertainment. But some big conglomerates are putting money behind pay TV, and the Federal Communications Commission is encouraging it.

It's unlikely, however, that pay TV will put the neighborhood movie theater out of business: people will always look for an excuse to get out of the house. What pay TV may do is force theaters to

ALICE DOESN'T LIVE HERE ANY MORE

change for the better. Eventually the competition may lead to such innovations in theaters as multiple projectors, 360-degree screens, and holograms.

Theaters will also take advantage of the new electronic technology. Imagine domestic satellites delivering movie by microwave to hundreds of theaters simultaneously, eliminating the need for multiple prints and those heavy film cans, and lowering the cost of distribution in the process. At the very least, pay TV will prompt theaters to replace

tattered screens, improve antiquated sound systems, and clean the filthy floors and seats more often. None of that will do Hollywood any harm.

"Hollywood's on the verge of the biggest money-making splurge in history," Marty Rackin concludes. "Owning three good negatives right now is better than owning six slot machines in Las Vegas. If I owned *Public Enemy, Little Caesar,* and *Casablanca,* I could retire tomorrow—and I'd be rich forever."

THE STING

A respected film critic recently made the charge that the Hollywood "system doesn't work any more, and it's not going to." Further, the critic charged, there is "a natural war in Hollywood between the businessmen and the artists." Industry people do read critics, I discovered during my visit here, and there is a kind of self-analysis going on. To some, the so-called system is working very well indeed, as proved by the fact that the national audience during the past year has jumped to 21 million a week, from 15 million the previous year. There are more "hits" than there have been in some time, and there is every expectation that many of the new films being fashioned will be hits, too.

Nevertheless, there is restlessness among the natives. I've encountered snickering on several levels over the wave of "disaster epics" that studios are currently pouring huge sums into. And there is dissatisfaction over the emphasis on action and adventure, to the neglect of other film-entertainment forms.

What about that supposed war between the artists and the businessmen? I talked to Paul Mazursky, a writer-director who has to be considered a film artist, in contradistinction to the kind of craftsman who fashions a *Poseidon Adventure* or a *Death Wish* for the satisfaction, if not the edification, of large audiences.

By the prevailing Hollywood manner of reckoning, Mazursky is a maverick. The first film he directed, *Bob & Carol & Ted & Alice,* was a big winner, both financially and critically. But, sadly, from "management's" point of view, he failed to follow through. He made a "personal" film called *Alex in Wonderland,* which lost MGM a quantity of money. Next came *Blume in Love,* which turned out to be something of a hit.

Two out of three is an excellent batting average in today's capricious movie market; yet Mazursky ran into trouble when he tried to get studio backing for *Harry and Tonto,* a project he had been devotedly harboring even prior to *Blume in Love.* He took it to Warner Brothers, the company that had released his previous film, and ran into cold shoulders.

"They," he said, meaning the management level, "aren't as stupid as they're sometimes made out to be. Movies are the only medium where the risk is as huge as it is. We, the so-called artists, are fools if we don't accept the fact that great sums of money are being risked when we're doing our own thing. Even so, I was really upset when Warner's rejected *Harry and Tonto.* I remember Ted Ashley, then the chairman of the board of the company, saying: 'Paul, I don't see the lines around the block.' Most of the others passed on it, too, but then Fox took a chance. What that meant was that the projected budget had to be pared down to the bone—and next to nothing for my fees."

Harry and Tonto is currently coming through nicely. Its story, about an elderly man and his cat and their odyssey across the country, got critical applause; audiences found the film amusing, wise, and touching. Fox will make a profit, and Mazursky will get his share.

"Frankly," he said, "if I were running one of these studios, I'd have had my doubts about making the story. The best bets for *them* are the films that stress violence and adventure. But if you keep doing that kind of thing, the level of taste will be lowered and that will hurt in the long run. If there's an answer to the dilemma, it's that the risks be shared and also the profits. You'd be surprised how many in this town are willing to make movies for the love of making movies."

Every time I visit Hollywood I find a change. On a previous visit Robert Altman was one of the hottest of the directors. He had made *M*A*S*H*, a stunning, surprise hit, and apparently he could do what he wanted from then on. In the estimation of critics, he continued to develop and grow into one of the most original of American film artists. But *Brewster McCloud, McCabe and Mrs. Miller, Images,* and *Thieves Like Us,* all provocative, often brilliant, failed to win large audiences. In order to make *California Split,* a dazzling display of film craftsmanship, acting, and clear-eyed perceptiveness that deals with this country's gambling fever, he had to wangle independent financing. He was indeed looked upon with suspicion by Hollywood management and also by Hollywood journalists. Joyce Haber, a columnist for the *Los Angeles Times,* termed it "the worst film I have seen," and *Daily Variety's* "Murf" came close to sharing that opinion.

Altman appeared to be unperturbed by these attacks. He has his own little setup on Westwood Boulevard, with office and editing space and a close-knit, devoted staff of assistants. I found him cutting together the massive, intricate project called *Nashville,* long enough to be shown as two separate films. The rushes he allowed me to see struck me as pure Americana, a fascinating evocation of the country-music scene.

"Oh, there may not be an obvious war going on between us and them," he said, "but it's there on a less conscious level. They don't trust us, and maybe, more important, they don't trust the audience. On the other hand, I can still make what I want to make. Not that it's easy. You have to spend time and waste your energies seeking out alternative methods of financing. Paramount released *Nashville,* but I had to get much of the money elsewhere. Meanwhile, I'm left alone, and after the thing is finished, we figure out how to handle it. But I'm happy. I love this picture. I can't even think of what I want to do next."

One of the town's most active agents, Jack Fields, told me: "One of my most wanted clients, Ned Beatty, went into Altman's picture for about a tenth of his customary fee, just for the chance to work with him. Actors know—and agents, too—that with a director like Bob, they're virtually guaranteed to be in a film of quality. with consequent help to their careers."

There are actors who will even work without pay, and, in one exceptional case, virtually pay for the privilege. Peter Falk, now of top rank in the television-star hierarchy through the "Columbo" series, received no salary for his appearance in *A Woman Under the Influence,* written and directed by John Cassavetes, Hollywood's most intractable maverick. Cassavetes, a star actor of considerable magnitude himself, spends most of his energies and resources making films that satisfy his need for expression. One million dollars was required for the making of *A Woman Under the Influence,* which also stars Cassavetes' wife, Gena Rowlands. He garnered half the amount by mortgaging their home and borrowing from friends. Peter Falk put up the other half-million.

I found Falk on the set of "Columbo" at Universal Studios. He hasn't appeared in a theatrical film since 1970, when he made *Husbands* with Cassavetes. His emergence to worldwide fame in "Columbo," however, has caused him to be showered with film scripts, almost all of which he has turned down. "I'd be the last one in the world," he said, "to reject a good role just because I thought the picture was going to make a lot of money. But I won't do films that strike me as silly, violent for the sake of violence, old-fashioned, or filled with sex for the sake of sex. I enjoy doing 'Columbo,' but every once in a while I feel the need to do something else, and John's picture gave me the opportunity. It's refreshing to work with people who are original and fertile.

"There's an emphasis on money here," he said, "a preoccupation with it that's not very healthy. Everyone should ease off it. I'm not strapped, so it's easy for me to say. But there are a lot of people who aren't strapped, and they'd be better off, the films would be better, if they backed off a bit from the buck. Sure there's room for action and adventure, but there's also enough of that. John and I went into this film without studio backing because we felt we could do it better if we did it on our own. The major problem is not that *they* watch over you, but if you can do it yourself it's more satisfying. Essentially it boils down to: Do you want to work for somebody, or do you want to work for yourself? It's tough for John and some of the others, but he gets the films done. And, frankly, I'm not sure that those who decide what properties are viable have the experience and ability to decide correctly. You don't have to try to gross 50 million every time out."

Falk and Cassavetes met on account of Elaine May, who, five years ago, had written a script called *Mikey and Nicky*. The film had two major roles, one of which Falk agreed to play. Both Miss May and Falk wanted Cassavetes for the other role. Falk set up the meeting and recounted the story, upon which Cassavetes said he'd do it without reading the script. "He explained," Falk said, " 'if Elaine May is directing and you're in it, I know it will make a good picture.' Then he said, 'I want you to do a picture with me.' I said, 'I want to see your script.' "

The Elaine May film was postponed, and Falk went to work with Cassavetes and Ben Gazzara on *Husbands,* a film regarded as exasperatingly long by some, and brilliant by others. "I worked for nothing," Falk said, "but because I had a third share in the picture, I received the largest pay check I'd yet received."

Since that time, Cassavetes, Falk, and Gazzara have become a tightly knit little group, as close and loyal as blood relatives. Gazzara is not in the new film, but he hangs around giving advice, counsel, and criticism, all of which Cassavetes listens to carefully and then proceeds to do as he deems right. One senses a pervasive love in the family, which also includes Gena Rowlands and Ben Gazzara's actress wife, Janice Rule.

While he doesn't see Hollywood as completely separated into two enemy camps, Cassavetes does see cross-purposes that make the artists and businessmen seem like violent enemies. He agreed that from the "management" point of view, he is a maverick. "There's a group of us," he said. Who makes up the group? "Altman, Elaine May, Paul Mazursky, Mel Brooks, Woody Allen, Francis Ford Coppola, some actors like Peter and Gena and Ben, George C. Scott, and others attempting to maintain their independence in a milieu gone crazy from the desire for huge profits and the power that comes from those profits.

"The main thing wrong with Hollywood is that the top level has lost sight of the fact that there are talented people here who have the need to express themselves personally, who feel themselves part of society, who regard their main job as expressing their version of what life is and what people are feeling. Our needs are expression. Their terrible needs are profits. So where do we fit into their terrible needs? We, as artists working in the most influential and expensive means of communication, feel we must express the spirit of the times. If curtailed by people in panic, the industry sooner or later will suffer. We can't survive without finances. We've both got to become more sensible and try to get together. We're not that far apart. I feel they're panicked. If they panic us, they'll never have anything.''

One cause of widespread discontent is the predominantly negotiating nature of the film industry. A look at the top level reveals most to be former lawyers or agents, whose expertise lies in the areas of taxes and contracts. The bargaining operates all the way up and down the line. Most of the major film companies are subsidiaries of large, diversified corporations. As subsidiaries, their jobs are to show profits for the benefit of stockholders and the financial health of the parent firm. It's only natural for management to examine those pictures that turn large profits and do more of the same.

''In the old days,'' said Paul Mazursky, ''there was continuity. A lot of talent had steady work writing, producing, acting in films, and those older films show a high level of craftsmanship. Masses of young people are discovering those films and finding how entertaining they are. It's not merely a nostalgia wave. So many of those films were *good*. But now it's a picture-by-picture thing. Each time a person makes a new deal, he's out to gouge the others, to get all he can or wants. It's the accepted way of doing things, and the industry is paying a price for the system that's developed.''

When *The Poseidon Adventure* made a huge profit, a similar formula was used for the large-scale *Towering Inferno*. When *Airport* became a historic money-maker, *Airport 1975* was put into the works. The argument of management is that it is giving the public what it obviously wants.

This formula doesn't mean, necessarily, that the management level doesn't recognize the talents of people like Elaine May, Altman, and Cassavetes. What it is more likely to fret about is their manner of working and their intractability. Miss May, currently cutting together *Mikey and Nicky,* has holed herself up in a small hotel off Sunset Boulevard, when she could more easily avail herself of the facilities of Paramount Studios, ten minutes away. She refuses to be hurried. She won't talk to the studio people. On the other hand, she'll get on the phone to Cassavettes and Falk, her stars and confederates, and talk a blue streak. ''It's going to be a wonderful picture,'' both Falk and Cassavetes say, with loving, comradely faith. The Paramount people don't know what to say. They haven't *seen* anything. And how can you judge, how can you say the overstretched budget will result in a profit, if you have nothing to go on *but* the talent of the filmmaker?

Yet, the mavericks have made films that served themselves and the audience, too. The maverick method, as opposed to the method desired by the ''system,'' has resulted in such films as *The Graduate, Easy Rider, Midnight Cowboy, M*A*S*H, The Heartbreak Kid, American Graffiti,* and *The Conversation.* Although some do talk of abandoning the system entirely and finding their own ways of reaching the public, the film-going public, the industry, and the art form itself would be badly served if the artists were further alienated. It's not so much that the system has to be abandoned as that it badly needs to be stretched.

REEL ONE

It was all technicolor
from bullets to nurses.
The guns gleamed like cars
and blood was as red
as the paint on dancers.
The screen shook with fire
and my bones whistled.
It was like life, but better.

I held my girl's hand,
in the deepest parts,
and we walked home, after,
with the snow falling,
but there wasn't much blue
in the drifts or corners:
just white and more white
and the sound track so dead
you could almost imagine
the trees were talking.

ADRIEN STOUTENBURG

good movie can take you out of your dull funk and the hopelessness that so often goes with slipping into a theatre; a good movie can make you feel alive again, in contact, not just lost in another city. Good movies make you care, make you believe in possibilities again. If somewhere in the Hollywood-entertainment world someone has managed to break through with something that speaks to you, then it isn't *all* corruption. The movie doesn't have to be great; it can be stupid and empty and you can still have the joy of a good performance, or the joy of just a good line. An actor's scowl, a small subversive gesture, a dirty remark that someone tosses off with a mock-innocent face, and the world makes a little bit of sense. Sitting there alone or painfully alone because those with you do not react as you do, you know there must be others perhaps in this very theatre or in this city, surely in other theatres in other cities, now, in the past or future, who react as you do. And because movies are the most total and encompassing art form we have, these reactions can seem the most personal, and maybe the most important, imaginable. The romance of movies is not just in those stories and those people on the screen but in the adolescent dream of meeting others who feel as you do about what you've seen. You do meet them, of course, and you know each other at once because you talk less about good movies than about what you love in bad movies.

ART VERSUS TECHNIQUE

There is so much talk now about the art of the film that we may be in danger of forgetting that most of the movies we enjoy are not works of art. Let's clear away a few misconceptions. Movies make hash of the schoolmarm's approach of how well the artist fulfilled his intentions. Whatever the original intention of the writers and director, it is usually supplanted, as the production gets under way, by the intention to make money—and the industry judges the film by how well it fulfills that intention. But if you could see the "artist's intentions" you'd probably wish you couldn't anyway. Nothing is so deathly to enjoyment as the relentless march of a movie to fulfill its obvious purpose. This is, indeed, almost a defining characteristic of the hack director, as distinguished from an artist.

The intention to make money is generally all too obvious. One of the excruciating comedies of our time is attending the new classes in cinema where the students may quite shrewdly and accurately interpret the plot developments in a mediocre movie in terms of manipulation for a desired response while the teacher tries to explain everything in terms of the creative artist working out his theme— as if the conditions under which a movie is made and the market for which it is designed were irrelevant, as if the latest product from Warners or Universal should be analyzed like a lyric poem.

People who are just getting "seriously interested" in film always ask a critic, "Why don't you talk about technique and 'the visuals' more?" The answer is that American movie technique is generally more like technology and it usually isn't very interesting. Hollywood movies often have the look of the studio that produced them—they have a studio style. Many current Warner films are noisy and have a bright look of cheerful ugliness, Universal films the cheap blur of money-saving processes, and so forth. Sometimes there is even a *spirit* that seems to belong to the studio. We can speak of the Paramount comedies of the Thirties or the Twentieth-Century Fox family entertainment of the Forties and CinemaScope comedies of the Fifties or the old MGM gloss, pretty much as we speak of Chevvies or Studebakers. These movies look alike, they move the same way, they have just about the same engines because of the studio policies and the *kind* of material the studio heads bought, the ideas they imposed, the way they had the films written, directed, photographed, and the labs where the prints were processed, and, of course, because of the presence of the studio stable of stars for whom the material was often purchased and shaped and who dominated the output of the studio. In some cases, as at Paramount in the Thirties, studio style was plain and rather tacky and the output—those comedies with Mary Boland and Mae West and Alison Skipworth and W. C. Fields—looks the better for it now. Those economical comedies weren't slowed down by a lot of fancy lighting or the adornments of "production values." Simply to be enjoyable, movies don't need a very high level of craftsmanship: wit, imagination, fresh subject matter, skillful performers, a good idea—either alone or in any combination—can more than compensate for lack of technical knowledge or a big budget.

Technique is hardly worth talking about unless it's used for something worth doing: that's why

most of the theorizing about the new art of television commercials is such nonsense. The effects are impersonal—dexterous, sometimes clever, but empty of art. It's because of their emptiness that commercials call so much attention to their camera angles and quick cutting—which is why people get impressed by "the art" of it. Movies are now often made in terms of what television viewers have learned to settle for. Despite a great deal that is spoken and written about young people responding visually, the influence of TV is to make movies visually less imaginative and complex. Television is a very noisy medium and viewers listen, while getting used to a poor quality of visual reproduction, to the absence of visual detail, to visual ob-

MY LITTLE CHICKADEE

viousness and overemphasis on simple composi-
tions, and to atrociously simplified and distorted
color systems. The shifting camera styles, the
movement, and the fast cutting of a film like
Finian's Rainbow—one of the better big productions—are like the "visuals" of TV commercials,
a disguise for static material, expressive of nothing
so much as the need to keep you from getting
bored and leaving. Men are now beginning their
careers as directors by working on commercials—
which, if one cares to speculate on it, may be
almost a one-sentence résumé of the future of
American motion pictures.

I don't mean to suggest that there is not such a
thing as movie technique or that craftsmanship

doesn't contribute to the pleasures of movies, but
simply that most audiences, if they enjoy the acting
and the "story" or the theme or the funny lines,
don't notice or care about how well or how badly
the movie is made, and because they don't care, a
hit makes a director a "genius" and everybody
talks about his brilliant technique (i.e., the technique of grabbing an audience).

ACTORS AND DIRECTORS

Just as there are good actors—possibly potentially
great actors—who have never become big stars
because they've just never been lucky enough to
get the roles they need (Brian Keith is a striking example) there are good directors who never got the
scripts and the casts that could make their reputa-
tions. The question people ask when they consider
going to a movie is not "How's it made?" but
"What's it about?" and that's a perfectly legitimate
question. (The next question—sometimes the first
—is generally, "Who's in it?" and that's a good,
honest question, too.) When you're at a movie, you
don't have to believe in it to enjoy it but you do
have to be interested. (Just as you have to be interested in the human material, too. Why should
you go see *another* picture with James Stewart?)
I don't want to see another samurai epic in exactly
the same way I never want to read *Kristin Lavrans-
datter*. Though it's conceivable that a truly great
movie director could make any subject interesting,
there are few such artists working in movies and if
they did work on unpromising subjects I'm not sure
we'd really enjoy the results even if we did *admire*
their artistry. (I recognize the greatness of sequences in several films by Eisenstein but it's a
rather cold admiration.) The many brilliant Italian
directors who are working within a commercial
framework on crime and action movies are ob-

MY LITTLE CHICKADEE

so many possible kinds and combinations of pleasure. One may be enthralled by Leontyne Price in *La Forza del Destino* even if one hasn't boned up on the libretto, or entranced by *The Magic Flute* even if one has boned up on the libretto, and a movie may be enjoyed for many reasons that have little to do with the story or the subtleties (if any) of theme or character. Unlike "pure" arts which are often defined in terms of what only they can do, movies are open and unlimited. Probably everything that can be done in movies can be done some other way, but—and this is what's so miraculous and so expedient about them—they can do almost anything any other art can do (alone or in combination) and they can take on some of the functions of exploration, journalism, of anthropology, of almost any branch of knowledge as well. We go to the movies for the variety of what they can provide, and for their marvelous ability to give us easily and inexpensively (and usually painlessly) what we can get from other arts also. They are a wonderfully *convenient* art.

THE HUMAN RESPONSE

We generally become interested in movies because we *enjoy* them and what we enjoy them for has little to do with what we think of as art. The movies we respond to, even in childhood, don't have the same values as the official culture supported at school and in the middle-class home. At the movies we get low life and high life, while David Susskind and the moralistic reviewers chastise us for not patronizing what they think we should, "realistic" movies that would be good for us—like *A Raisin in the Sun,* where we could learn the lesson that a black family can be as dreary as a white family. Movie audiences will take a lot of garbage, but it's pretty hard to make us queue up for pedagogy. At the movies we want a different kind of truth,

viously not going to be of any great interest unless they get a chance to work on a subject we care about.

When we are children, though there are categories of films we don't like—documentaries generally (they're too much like education) and, of course, movies especially designed for children—by the time we can go on our own we have learned to avoid them. Children are often put down by adults when the children say they enjoyed a particular movie; adults who are short on empathy are quick to point out aspects of the plot or theme that the child didn't understand, and it's easy to humiliate a child in this way. But it is one of the glories of eclectic arts like opera and movies that they include something that surprises us and registers with us as funny or accurate or maybe amazing, maybe even amazingly beautiful. We get little things even in mediocre and terrible movies—José Ferrer sipping his booze through a straw in *Enter Laughing,* Scott Wilson's hard scary all-American-boy-you-can't-reach face cutting through the pretensions of *In Cold Blood* with all its fancy bleak cinematography. We got, and still have embedded in memory, Tony Randall's surprising depth of feeling in *The Seven Faces of Dr. Lao,* Keenan Wynn and Moyna Macgill in the lunch-counter sequence of *The Clock,* John W. Bubbles on the dance floor in *Cabin in the Sky.* Though the director may have been responsible for releasing it, it's the human material we react to most and remember longest. The art of the performers stays fresh for us, their beauty as beautiful as ever. There are so many kinds of things we get—the hangover sequence wittily designed for the CinemaScope screen in *The Tender Trap,* the atmosphere of the newspaper offices in *The Luck of Ginger Coffey,* the automat gone mad in *Easy Living.* Do we need to lie and shift things to false terms—like those who have to say Sophia Loren is a great actress as if her *acting* had made her a star? Wouldn't we rather watch her than better actresses because she's so incredibly charming and because she's probably the greatest model the world has ever known? There are great moments—Angela Lansbury singing "Little Yellow Bird" in *Dorian Gray.* (I don't think I've ever had a friend who didn't also treasure that girl and that song.) And there are absurdly right little moments —in *Saratoga Trunk* when Curt Bois says to Ingrid Bergman, "You're very beautiful," and she says, "Yes, isn't it lucky?" And those things have closer relationships to art than what the schoolteachers told us was true and beautiful. Not that the works we studied in school weren't often great (as we discovered *later*) but that what the teachers told us to

admire them for (and if current texts are any indication, are still telling students to admire them for) was generally so false and prettified and moralistic that what might have been moments of pleasure in them, and what might have been cleansing in them, and subversive, too, had been coated over.

Part of the fun of movies is in seeing "what everybody's talking about," and if people are flocking to a movie, or if the press can con us into thinking that they are, then ironically, there is a sense in which we want to see it, even if we suspect we won't enjoy it, because we want to know what's going on. Even if it's the worst inflated pompous trash that is the most talked about (and it usually is) and even if that talk is manufactured, we want to see the movies because so many people fall for whatever is talked about that they make the advertisers' lies true. Movies absorb material from the culture and the other arts so fast that some films that have been widely *sold* become culturally and sociologically important whether they are good movies or not. Movies like *Morgan!* or *Georgy Girl* or the *The Graduate*—aesthetically trivial movies which, however, because of the ways some people react to them, enter into the national bloodstream—become cultural and psychological equivalents of watching a political convention—to observe what's going on. And though this has little to do with the art of movies, it has a great deal to do with the appeal of movies.

An analyst tells me that when his patients are not talking about their personal hangups and their immediate problems they talk about the situations and characters in movies like *The Graduate* or *Belle de Jour* and they talk about them with as much personal involvement as about their immediate problems. I have elsewhere suggested that this way of reacting to movies as psychodrama used to be considered a pre-literate way of reacting but that now those considered "post-literate" are reacting like pre-literates. The high school and college students identifying with Georgy Girl or Dustin Hoffman's Benjamin are not that different from the stenographer who used to live and breathe with the Joan Crawford-working girl and worry about whether that rich boy would really make her happy —and considered her pictures "great." They don't see the movie as a movie but as part of the soap opera of their lives. The fan magazines used to encourage this kind of identification; now the *advanced* mass media encourage it, and those who want to sell to youth use the language of "just let it flow over you." The person who responds this way does not respond more freely but less freely and less fully than the person who is aware of what is well done and what badly done in a movie, who can accept some things in it and reject others, who uses all his senses in reacting, not just his emotional vulnerabilities.

TRASH VERSUS ART

When you're young the odds are very good that you'll find something to enjoy in almost any movie. But as you grow more experienced, the odds change. I saw a picture a few years ago that was the sixth version of material that wasn't much to start with. Unless you're feebleminded, the odds get worse and worse. We don't go on reading the same kind of manufactured novels—pulp Westerns or detective thrillers, say—all of our lives, and we don't want to go on and on looking at movies about cute heists by comically assorted gangs. The problem with a popular art form is that those who want something more are in a hopeless minority compared with the millions who are always seeing it for the first time, or for the reassurance and gratification of seeing the conventions fulfilled again. Probably a large part of the older audience gives up

movies for this reason—simply that they've seen it before. And probably this is why so many of the best movie critics quit. They're wrong when they blame it on the movies going bad; it's the odds becoming so bad, and they can no longer bear the many tedious movies for the few good moments and the tiny shocks of recognition. Some become too tired, too frozen in fatigue, to respond to what *is* new. Others who *do* stay awake may become too demanding for the young who are seeing it all for the first hundred times. The critical task is necessarily comparative, and younger people do not truly know what is new. And despite all the chatter about the media and how smart the young are, they're incredibly naïve about mass culture—perhaps *more* naïve than earlier generations (though I don't know why). Maybe watching all that television hasn't done so much for them as they seem to think; and when I read a young intellectual's appreciation of *Rachel, Rachel* and come to "the mother's passion for chocolate bars is a superb symbol for the second coming of childhood" I know the writer is still in his first childhood, and I wonder if he's going to come out of it.

One's moviegoing tastes and habits change—I still like in movies what I always liked but now, for example, I really want documentaries. After all the years of stale stupid acted-out stories, with less and less for me in them, I am desperate to know something, desperate for facts, for information, for faces of nonactors and for knowledge of how people live —for revelations, not for the little bits of show-business detail worked up for us by show-business minds who got them from the same movies we're tired of.

But the big change is in our *habits*. If we make any kind of decent, useful life for ourselves we have less need to run from it to those diminishing pleasures of the movies. When we go to the movies we want something good, something sustained, we don't want to settle for just a bit of something, because we have other things to do. If life at home is more interesting, why go to the movies? And the theaters frequented by true moviegoers—those perennial displaced persons in each city, the loners and the losers—depress us. Listening to them—and they are often more audible than the sound track—as they cheer the cons and jeer the cops, we may still share their disaffection, but it's not enough to keep us interested in cops and robbers. A little nose-thumbing isn't enough. If we've grown up at the movies we know that good work is continuous not with the academic, respectable tradition but with the glimpses of something good in trash, but we want the subversive gesture carried to the domain of discovery. Trash has given us an appetite for art.

CRIME MOVIES

All horrors are grist for the Hollywood mill, but cheap exploitation films don't disguise their purposes, whereas an expensive, "responsible" film like *The Boston Strangler,* with real stars like Henry Fonda and Tony Curtis, deals with brutality and madness tastefully, in safe, academic terms, thus offering perversions with polite reassurances. It's money that makes a film look responsible.

Indirectly, new crime movies are begotten by old ones; the pulp novels that the movie companies buy for this kind of picture are written by fast writers, who synthesize old movies for their plots and characters. New kinds of crime rarely appear in them; the authors generally don't know any more about crime than one can learn from old movies. Nor is it likely that the producers would take a chance on a crime script that didn't resemble earlier pictures, and so crime movies shrivel in interest. But even within the limited terrain of the straight robbery picture derived from other robbery

THE ROARING TWENTIES

pictures it's possible to do a workmanlike job—to present the occupational details of crime accurately (or convincingly), to assemble the gang so that we get a sense of the kinds of people engaged in crime and what their professional and nonprofessional lives are like. A good crime movie generally has a sordid, semi-documentary authenticity about criminal activities—big ones and petty, queasy ones—plus the nervous excitement of what it might be like to rob and to tangle with the law. After a run of spoof heists, robbery pictures are coming out again without self-parody. *The Split* is of the same genre. It is about a robbery planned to coincide with a professional football game.

In a good robbery picture, the chases and the violence are integral to the story; in a poor robbery picture they're just thrown in to relieve the bore-

CHITTY CHITTY BANG BANG

dom, and you may be grateful for them because you know that's all the excitement you're going to get. Jim Brown, as the leader of the gang, selects his men in a series of brutal tests—one act of mayhem after another—that are obviously designed merely to give the picture a big opening, since they have no relationship to the skills that are later required of them. After the robbery, when the money is stolen from the men, they beat and torture Brown in another implausible sequence. They're not so stupid and unprofessional as to suppose he would have taken the money and waited around to be beaten; clearly, somebody thought it would be good for the box office to have the hero tortured. The action sequences in the James Bond films and in spoofs in general are not plausible, yet one

doesn't mind, and, conceivably, action sequences in a "serious" heist film could be so well done that one wouldn't mind implausibility in them, either. But in *The Split* the director, Gordon Flemyng, tries a lot of flashy stuff that doesn't work.

MOVIES FOR CHILDREN

It's one of the paradoxes of movie business that the movies designed expressly for children are generally the ones that frighten them most. I have never heard children screaming in fear at any of those movies we're always told they should be protected from as they screamed at *Bambi* and *Dumbo*. Bambi's mother is murdered, Dumbo's mother is goaded to madness and separated from Dumbo;

these movies really hit children where it counts. And here we are again in *Chitty Chitty Bang Bang,* with its climax of a child-catcher (Robert Helpmann) who lures hungry children with promises of sweets, traps them right before the eyes of helpless adults, and throws them into prison. What a sweet bit of whimsy! This musical for children is almost sadistically ill-planned: it runs a hundred and fifty-six minutes, plus intermission, and almost all the fantasy material is in the last hour. That means that the small children (and who else wants to see it?) will be restless, exhausted, overfed, sticky, and irritable long before they even get a chance to become frightened and upset. Do the men who concoct these entertainments ever consider the simple logistics of what parents go through before, during, and after a three-hour movie?

This ten-million-dollar musical fantasy for children has a desperate jollity; everybody has been doing his damnedest and everything has gone hopelessly wrong. The script, by Roald Dahl and the director Ken Hughes (from Ian Fleming's volume of stories about an Edwardian motorcar which makes noises that sound like "chitty chitty bang bang"), tries to be fanciful. The writers try to appeal to kids with the kind of cheerlessly cheerful "imaginative fantasy" that falls flat between comic strip and fairy tale, and they try to appeal to adults with a jokey tone of complicity that keeps saying: Look at those precious children, and doesn't everybody love harmless eccentrics? They might as well have gone the rest of the way and put canned laughter on the sound track. The movie needs it, because the writers have failed to make the eccentrics into characters. And Ken Hughes directs in that "Isn't this humorous?" style of Ken Annakin's *Those Magnificent Men in Their Flying Machines,* only much worse. I have some residual affection for Dick Van Dyke, but I don't understand why, so

PETER RABBIT AND THE TALES OF BEATRIX POTTER

early in his career, when he should be fighting for good roles, he has sunk to family pictures of the sort that actors fall back on when they're finished. He *is* ingratiating; he shouldn't *act* ingratiating. He has become a daddy before he needed to.

Maybe it's just because the action in *Chitty Chitty Bang Bang* eventually shifts from England to a Bavarian kingdom called Vulgaria, where people talk in comic German accents, but the whole thing seemed to be an Aryan nightmare. Sally Ann Howes (as Truly Scrumptious) has that cold "princess" look that the movie moguls have always foisted on us as beauty. She's the female equivalent of the "handsome" Hudsons and Pecks who are cast as "the hero" because they don't project enough character or interest for anything else. She looks absolutely in place when she's pretending to be the mechanical doll on a German music box. This bland operetta of a movie is hardly in a position to satirize Vulgaria. German dialect humor has never been very witty—it's always broad and forced—but Anna Quayle manages to bring off a duet with Gert Frobe, called "Chu-Chi Face," that is the high point of the movie. Miss Quayle is getting to be a picture-redeemer, the way Angela Lansbury (whom she somewhat resembles) used to be. Other good points are the first sight of Ken Adam's two big sets for the Scrumptious Candy Cookery, and the little-girl heroine (Heather Ripley), a storybook girl who is serenely, unconscionably beautiful. The magical flying-floating car itself is elegant when seen from underneath in the air, but the technical processes are a disgrace; when children have waited so long to be carried aloft in imagination, such clumsy fakery seems cruel. The con-struction of the Pushmi-Pullyu and the Great Pink Sea Snail in *Doctor Dolittle* were also pathetic. *Finian's Rainbow,* with fewer magical effects, had more magical feeling. Big, expensive movie fantasies used to be very proud of their technical perfection, but perhaps fantasy must always be the imaginative expression of one person, whether a storyteller or a designer or a director, and the factory methods of the big, new, overanxious productions don't work. It may be that modern movie-making methods take the magic out of magic.

MOVIE WESTERNS

There has always been a basic ambivalence in the Westerns that dealt with Indian vs. white. Even when the Indians were represented as betrayed and goaded beyond endurance—and they often have

SHANE

been represented that way—the audience, in the crunch of the final battle, rooted for the white settlers huddled against their wagons while the flaming arrows of "the savages" flew toward them. The hero and heroine would survive, the Indians would be wiped out or driven off. This ambivalence is the plague of the Western: ultimately, the whites are the good guys and the Indians the bad guys. If we were appalled during the Second World War by all those movies that turned the issues of the war into a simple contest between us (good, decent, human) and them (evil, cruel, treacherous, fanatic, psychopathic, inhuman), and if we refuse to go to see something like *The Green Berets* because the standard movie reduction of the issues to good and evil and the dehumanization of the enemy are repulsive to us, then maybe we should ask: What's going on in *The Stalking Moon,* with that Apache in his bestial garb? Because if he's a symbol, I don't think it's

for the Apaches of the Southwest. I think he's a stand-in.

Here is what *Life* says about the movie: "It is an examination in archetype of good and evil locked in a death grapple. It has the simplicity and fascination of a myth dredged up from the unconscious of the race. It is, in this simplicity, what movies are all about." People may think this is what movies are all about because this conflict between good guys and bad guys is what moved them as children and they may have the desire to be gripped the same way when they go to movies as adults. They feel it's the real thing—"pure movie" —when it's a basic morality play. If the monster were not an Apache in a bearskin but a Jew dressed in money, that could tap "the unconscious," too. And if the monster were a naked black man carrying a spear, the movie could score a knockout at the "unconscious" level. The Apache has been

HIGH NOON

stripped of all humanity in order to make him function as pure bad guy, and then we are told that the child must make a *choice* between the cultures of his mother and his father, as if between his good and evil heritages. The child's soul is being battled for, and his final winning over to his mother's culture becomes the moral aim of the picture. The implication is that if his Indian side wins, his future will be murderous and the country will be in turmoil, but if his white side wins, all will go well for the country.

One foundation executive told me that he was quite upset that his teen-agers had chosen to go to *Bonnie and Clyde* rather than with him to *Closely Watched Trains.* He took it as a sign of lack of maturity. I think his kids made an honest choice, and not only because *Bonnie and Clyde* is the better movie, but because it is closer to us, it has some of the qualities of direct involvement that make us care about movies. But it's understandable that it's easier for us, as Americans, to see *art* in foreign films than in our own, because of how we, as Americans, think of art. Art is still what ladies and foundations believe in, it's civilized and refined, cultivated and serious, cultural, beautiful, European, Oriental: It's what America isn't, and it's especially what American movies are not. Still, if those kids had chosen *Wild in the Streets* over *Closely Watched Trains* I would think that was a sound and honest choice, too, even though *Wild in the Streets* is in most ways a terrible picture. It connects with their lives in an immediate even if a grossly frivolous way, and if we don't go to movies for excitement, if, even as children, we accept the cultural standards of refined adults, if we have so little drive that we accept "good taste," then we will probably never really begin to care about movies at all.

JUDITH CRIST

journalist and movie critic

Change is part of living, and making a scapegoat of television or movies does not solve the problem. The roots lie deep within the family and our society. We cannot settle for a surface solution, or leave it to legislators to solve what is a personal problem.

Look around you, beyond the television set and the movie screen. I was just glancing through one of the world's most respected newspapers, one which has joined others in condemning the exploitation of prurience and lust. My eye caught an ad, for a chic, expensive store, with the headline: ''An Orgy for Foot Fetishists.'' It was an ad for a plain, old-fashioned shoe sale.

THE CHICAGO TRIBUNE

Sweden, as everyone knows, allows the most graphic sex pictures on its movie screen and exports sexploitation features. But that doesn't mean that anything goes on the Swedish screen. Consider the plight of *Tom Sawyer,* the G-rated American musical. In one scene, Injun Joe throws a knife at Tom—and Swedish censors probably will cut it out. The reason: The Swedes abhor violence as much as they love sex. Sweden once forbade anyone under 12 to view the saccharine superhit *The Sound of Music* because it was believed that young children would be unduly scared during scenes in which Nazis chase the Von Trapp kids from their home.

Have the Movies Gone Too Far?
Some Differing Opinions

BERGEN EVANS

professor of English at Northwestern University

I am much more concerned with sadism than with sex in the entertainment media. The movies have always settled all human problems with a quick right to the jaw—and perhaps this has led many of our young people to assume that the answer to any problem is to smash things up.

JACK VALENTI

president of the Motion Picture Association of America

We simply cannot discard the right of the artist to film what he chooses, in the way he chooses. Sometimes to shock is to seize the truth, and sometimes to unsettle is to make visible a revelation. Moreover, one must buy a ticket to see a movie; no one is forced to enter a movie theater.

We have created a film-rating system which tells parents in advance what kind of movie is playing at the local theater, and allows them to judge whether or not they should take their children. This system rates films on the acceptability of the material, as it pertains to children. With the cooperation of the National Association of Theater Owners, viewing of certain films is restricted to adults.

But even this film rating does not repeal the basic rules of public decency. No responsible person ought ever to defend the fakery of those who construct vulgarity and call it art. When discipline and discretion disappear, we will have gone culturally berserk. There is such a thing as good taste, and if one has to ask what it is, he plainly doesn't have it.

The majority of creative film-makers and executives are allied in their judgment that excellence, not hokum, is what endures. But the public has a responsibility, too: the obligation to stay away from trash and give their patronage to quality.

A NEW
UNDERSTANDING
OF MEDIA

THE NEW LANGUAGES

Marshall McLuhan and Edmund Carpenter

ENGLISH is a mass medium. ALL languages are mass media. The new mass media—film, radio, TV—are new 1ne languages, their grammars as yet unknown. Each codifies reality differently; each conceals a unique metaphysics. Linguists tell us it's possible to say anything in any language if you use enough words or images, but there's rarely time; the natural course is for a culture to exploit its media biases.

WRITING didn't record oral language; it was a new language, which the spoken word came to imitate. 2wo Where preliterate man imposed form diffidently, temporarily on the tip of his tongue, in the living situation—the printed word was inflexible, permanent; it embalmed truth for posterity.

This embalming process froze language. The word became a static symbol, applicable to and separate from that which it symbolized. The manuscript page gave way to uniform type, the black-and-white page, read silently, alone. The format of the book favored lineal expression, for the argument ran like a thread from cover to cover. This was not true of great poetry and drama, which retained multi-perspective, but it was true of most books, particularly texts, histories, autobiographies, novels.

THE newspaper format brought an end to book culture. It offers short, discrete articles that give important facts 3hree first and then taper off to incidental details, which may be, and often are, eliminated by the make-up man. The fact that reporters cannot control the length of their articles means that, in writing them, emphasis can't be placed on structure, at least in the traditional linear sense, with climax or conclusion at the end. Everything has to be captured in the headline; from there it goes down the pyramid to incidentals. In fact there is often more in the headline than in the article; occasionally, no article at all accompanies the banner headline.

The disorder of the newspaper throws the reader into a producer role. The reader has to process the news himself; he has to co-create, to cooperate in the creation of the work. The newspaper format calls for the direct participation of the consumer.

In magazines, where a writer more frequently controls the length of his article, he can, if he wishes, organize it in traditional style, but the majority don't. An increasingly popular presentation is the printed symposium, which is little more than collected opinions, pro and con. The magazine format as a whole opposes lineality; its pictures lack tenses. In *Life*, extremes are juxtaposed: space ships and prehistoric monsters, Flemish monasteries and dope addicts. It creates a sense of urgency and uncertainty: the next page is unpredictable. One encounters rapidly a riot in Teheran, a Hollywood marriage, a two-headed calf, a party on Jones beach, all sandwiched between ads. The eye takes in the page as a whole (readers may pretend this isn't so, but the success of advertising suggests it is), and the page—indeed, the whole magazine—becomes a single structure where association, though not causal, is often lifelike.

The same is true of the other new languages. Both radio and TV offer short, unrelated programs, interrupted between and within by commercials. I say "interrupted," being myself an anachronism of book culture, but my children don't regard them as interruptions, as breaking continuity. Rather, they regard them as part of a whole, and their reaction is neither one of annoyance nor one of indifference. The ideal news broadcast has half a dozen speakers from as many parts of the world on as many subjects. The London correspondent doesn't comment on what the Washington correspondent has just said; he hasn't even heard him.

4our   THE child is right in not regarding commercials as interruptions. For the only time anyone smiles on TV is in commercials. The rest of life, in news broadcasts and soap operas, is presented as so horrible that the only way to get through life is to buy this product: then you'll smile. Aesop never wrote a clearer fable. It's heaven and hell brought up to date: Hell in the headline, Heaven in the ad. Without the other, neither has meaning.

This is especially true of ads that never present an ordered, sequential, rational argument but simply present the product associated with desirable things or attitudes. Thus Coca-Cola is shown held by a beautiful blonde, who sits in a Cadillac, surrounded by bronze, muscular admirers, with the sun shining overhead. By repetition these elements become associated, in our minds, into a pattern of sufficient cohesion so that one element can magically evoke the others. If we think of ads as designed solely to sell products, we miss their main effect: to increase pleasure in the consumption of the product. Coca-Cola is far more than a cooling drink; the consumer participates, vicariously, in a much larger experience. In Africa, in Melanesia, to drink a Coke is to participate in the American way of life.

EACH medium selects its ideas. TV is a tiny box into which people are crowded and must live; film gives us the wide world. With its huge screen, film is perfectly suited for social drama, Civil War panoramas, the sea, land erosion, Cecil B. DeMille spectaculars. In contrast, the TV screen has room for two, at the most three, faces comfortably. TV is closer to stage, yet different. Paddy Chayefsky writes:

The theatre audience is far away from the actual action of the drama. They cannot see the silent reactions of the players. They must be told in a loud voice what is going on. The plot movement from one scene to another must be marked, rather than gently shaded as is required in television. In television, however, you can dig into the most humble, ordinary relationships: the relationship of bourgeois children to their mother, of middle-class husband to his wife, of white-collar father to his secretary—in short, the relationship of the people. We relate to each other in an incredibly complicated manner. There is far more exciting drama in the reasons why a man gets married than in why he murders someone. The man who is unhappy in his job, the wife who thinks of a lover, the girl who wants to get into television, your father, your mother, sister, brothers, cousins, friends—all these are better subjects for drama than Iago. What makes a man ambitious? Why does a girl always try to steal her kid sister's boy friends? Why does your uncle attend his annual class reunion faithfully every year? Why do you always find it depressing to visit your father? These are the substances of good television drama; and the deeper you probe into and examine the twisted, semi-formed complexes of emotional entanglements, the more exciting your writing becomes.

THE appearance of a new medium often frees older media for creative effort. They no longer have to serve the interests of power and profit. Elia Kazan, discussing the American theatre, says:

Take 1900–1920. The theatre flourished all over the country. It had no competition. The box office boomed. The top original fare it had to offer was *The Girl of the Golden West.* Its bow to culture was fusty productions of Shakespeare. . . . Came the moving picture. The theatre had to be better or go under. It got better. It got so spectacularly better so fast that in 1920–1930 you wouldn't have recognized it. Perhaps it was an accident that Eugene O'Neill appeared at that moment—but it was no accident that in that moment of strange competition, the theatre had room for him. Because it was disrupted and hard pressed, it made room for his experiments, his unheard-of subjects, his passion, his power. There was room for him to grow to his full stature. And there was freedom for the talents that came after his.

7even YET a new language is rarely welcomed by the old. The oral tradition distrusted writing, manuscript culture was contemptuous of printing, book culture hated the press, that "slag-heap of hellish passions," as one 19th century scholar called it. A father, protesting to a Boston newspaper about crime and scandal, said he would rather see his children "in their graves while pure in innocence, than dwelling with pleasure upon these reports, which have grown so bold."

A new language lets us see with the fresh, sharp eyes of the child; it offers the pure joy of discovery. I was recently told a story about a Polish couple who, though long resident in Toronto, retained many of the customs of their homeland. Their son despaired of ever getting his father to buy a suit cut in style or getting his mother to take an interest in Canadian life. Then he bought them a TV set, and in a matter of months a major change took place. One evening the mother remarked that "Edith Piaf is the latest thing on Broadway," and the father appeared in "the kind of suit executives wear on TV." For years the father had passed this same suit in store windows and seen it both in advertisements and on living men, but not until he saw it on TV did it become meaningful. This same statement goes for all media: each offers a unique presentation of reality, which when new has a freshness and clarity that is extraordinarily powerful.

This is especially true of TV. We say, "We have a radio" but "We have television"—as if something had happened to us. It's no longer "The skin you love to touch" but "The Nylon that loves to touch you." We don't watch TV; it watches us: it guides us. Magazines and newspapers no longer convey "information" but offer ways of seeing things. They have abandoned realism as too easy: they substitute themselves for realism. *Life* is totally advertisements: its articles package and sell emotions and ideas just as its paid ads sell commodities.

8ight CURRENT confusion over the respective roles of the new media comes largely from a misconception of their function. They are art-forms, not substitutes for human contact. Insofar as they attempt to usurp speech and personal, living relations, they harm. This, of course, has long been one of the problems of book culture, at least during the time of its monopoly of Western middle-class thought. But this was never a legitimate function of books, nor of any other medium. Whenever a medium goes claim jumping, trying to work areas where it is ill-suited, conflicts occur with other media, or, more accurately, between the vested interests controlling each. But, when media simply exploit their own formats, they become complementary and cross-fertile.

178

Some people who have no one around talk to cats, and you can hear their voices in the next room, and they sound silly, because the cat won't answer, but that suffices to maintain the illusion that their world is made up of living people, while it is not. Mechanized mass media reverse this: now mechanical cats talk to humans. There's no genuine feedback.

This charge is often leveled by academicians at the new media, but it holds equally for print. The open-mouthed, glaze-eyed TV spectator is merely the successor of the passive, silent, lonely reader whose head moved back and forth like a shuttlecock.

WHEN we read, another person thinks for us: we merely repeat his mental process. The greater part of the work of thought is done for us. This is why it relieves us to take up a book after being occupied by our own thoughts. In reading, the mind is only the playground for another's ideas. People who spend most of their lives in reading often lose the capacity for thinking, just as those who always ride forget how to walk. Some people read themselves stupid. Chaplin did a wonderful take-off of this in *City Lights*, when he stood up on a chair to eat the endless confetti that he mistook for spaghetti.

9ine

EACH medium, if its bias is properly exploited, reveals and communicates a unique aspect of reality, of truth. Each offers a different perspective, a way of seeing an otherwise hidden dimension of reality. It's not a question of one reality being true, the others distortions. One allows us to see from here, another from there, a third from still another perspective; taken together they give us a more complete whole, a greater truth. New essentials are brought to the fore, including those made invisible by the "blinders" of old languages.

10n

THE MEDIA

MARSHALL McLUHAN

All media are extensions of some

human faculty–psychic or physical.

The wheel

...is an extension of the foot

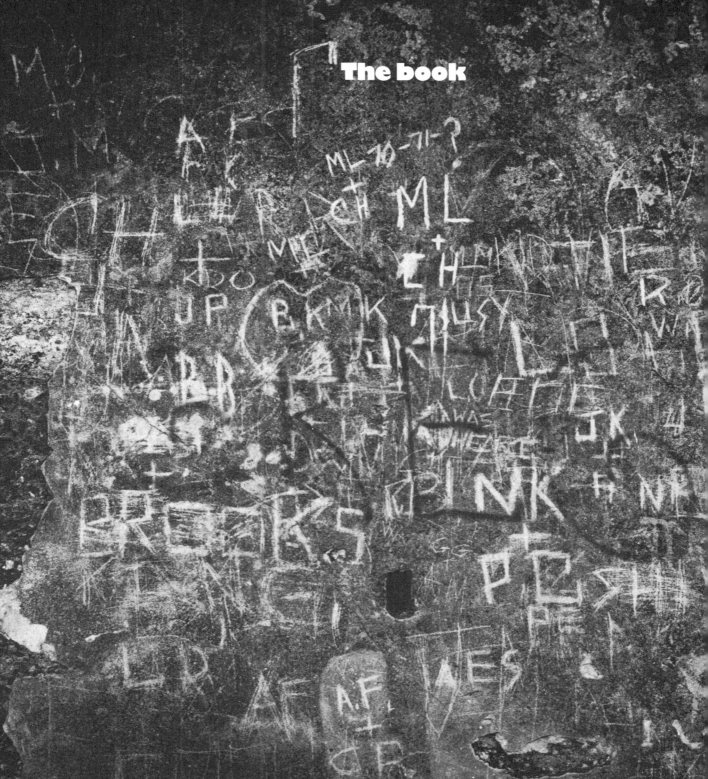

The book

is an extension of the eye...

Clothing, an extension of the skin...

electric circuitry, an extension of

the central nervous system

Media, by altering the environment, evoke in us
unique ratios of sense perceptions. The extension of any one sense alters the way we
think and act—the way we perceive the world.

When

these

ratios

change,

men change.

THE CITY

no longer exists,

except as a cultural ghost for tourists.

Any highway eatery with its TV set,

newspaper, and magazine is

as cosmopolitan as New York or Paris.

MARSHALL McLUHAN

arshall McLuhan's *Understanding Media* has possibly the least catchy title for an important book since *Principia Mathematica;* however, it is somewhat easier to read once you have got the hang of it.

The hard part is getting into it. One school of thought says that you should start at page 77, or wherever, and then sit through it again the way you do when you come in on the middle of a movie. Another holds that you should skim through it once, saving your thunderstruck (or indignant) marginal notations for the second time around. The trouble with this is that skimming McLuhan is like trying to fill a tea cup from a firehose; there is likely to be no second time.

It is quite possible, I think, to start cheerfully at the beginning, provided one has some notion going in of what McLuhan is up to. To begin with, what Professor McLuhan means by a "medium" is any extension of man—whether it be a book, an automobile, an electric light bulb, television, or clothes. His theory is that the media a man uses to extend his senses and his faculties will determine what he is, rather than the other way around. To give a simple example: a car is certainly an extension of a man's legs. Moreover, when he drives a car he has in a sense amputated his legs. He is an amputee just as surely as though he had lost his legs first and then looked for a way to get around.

Similarly, by wearing clothes a man eliminates a good many of the functions that his body would have to perform were he naked. Let us consider this proposition in its most extreme form: a native living at the Equator and an Eskimo. The tropical native, because he is naked, has no means of re-taining body heat; therefore he must eat constantly or die. He can starve to death in a day or two. The Eskimo, heavily furred, keeps his body heat and can go without food for weeks if necessary. This is not, of course, to suggest that the Indians of the upper Amazon would be better off with long johns and fur coats, or that Eskimos would be better supermarket customers if they ran around in the buff, but that the media a society uses or is forced to use will determine what it is and how it behaves.

Incidentally, we are used to thinking of clothes as something we wear next to our bodies. Objectively, however, clothes are an extension of our skins. For a naked tribesman, the jungle is his clothes. When one of us runs around naked in a heated room, the room itself is clothes, an extension of our skin, a medium. You recall that earlier I said that any medium will tend to amputate the function which it extends? You can test this very easily by walking into a warm house on a cold day. The first thing you do is take off your overcoat.

Now, to carry this one step further, any new medium or extension of man constitutes a new environment which controls what people who live within it do, the way they think, and the way they act. If you wonder why the Russians behave and react differently from us, part of the answer is probably that until quite recently they lived in a pre-literate society, whereas ours has been literate for a very long time. They are historically ear-oriented whereas we are eye-oriented. There is a great difference.

A man who cannot read will pick up all information about what has gone on before and what is happening outside his field of vision by hearing about it. His world will therefore be more diffused and kaleidoscopic than that of the literate, eye-oriented man because the ear cannot be focused and the eye can.

The process of reading—which I suppose we could define as using our eyes to learn about things we cannot see—is dependent on this unique ability of the eye to focus and follow sequentially. Few people have been able to read at any given time during the past few thousand years since writing was invented. It is only recently, since Gutenberg, that literacy has become the general environment for even a small part of the world. Latin America, Eastern and Southern Europe, Asia, and Africa are still either pre-literate or Johnny-come-latelies to reading; their environmental structures are still ear-oriented.

The differences between literate and pre-literate societies are enormous. Not the least of these differences is technological. Mass production did not begin with the industrial revolution, but with the first printed page that Gutenberg pulled off his press. For the first time, items could be mass produced so that one was indistinguishable from another and all of the same value. This was quite a break-through after millennia of making one object at a time and each different from the other.

But more important was the environment imposed by the medium of print itself: one word after the other, one sentence after another, one paragraph after another, one page after another; one thing at a time in a logical, connected line. The effects of this linear thinking are deep and influence every facet of a literate society such as our own.

An ear-oriented society, on the other hand, will neither act nor react in this one-thing-at-a-time fashion, but will tend to receive and express many experiences simultaneously. It is the difference between our baseball, which is surely one thing after another in a logical sequence, and their soccer which is everything happening at once. Perhaps it is why most of the best chess players—and chess is surely everything happening at once, with millions and millions of simultaneous possibilities—come from pre-literate countries. Or why so many atomic physicists are either Hungarians or Americans in their early twenties. Or why teen-agers can listen to the radio full blast, study, and put their hair up in curlers at the same time.

I mention teen-agers because it is becoming abundantly apparent that they are not, as we previously thought, going through a phase. They are a different breed of cat entirely. All sorts of reasons have been given for their emergence as a distinct group, among them prosperity and lack of discipline. And what the hell, I was young once myself. I *was*—but not like that. For one thing I wasn't as smart as that. Also, this teen-age revolution has been going on for quite a few years now and the early crop is getting up in its late twenties. And I wasn't like them when I was twenty-six either.

Well, what has happened? McLuhan's theory is that this is the first generation of the electronic age. He says they are different because the medium that controls their environment is not print—one thing at a time, one thing after another—as it has been for five hundred years. It is television, which is everything happening at once, instantaneously, and enveloping.

A child who gets his environment training on television—and very few nowadays do not—learns the same way any member of a pre-literate society learns: from the direct experience of his eyes and ears, without Gutenberg for a middle man. Of course they do learn how to read too, but it is a secondary discipline, not primary as it is with their elders. When it comes to shaping sensory perceptions, I'm afraid that Master Gutenberg just isn't in the same class with General Sarnoff or Doctor Stanton.

Despite the uproar over inferior or inept television fare, McLuhan does not think that the program content of television has anything to do with the real changes TV has produced; no more than whether a book is trashy or a classic has anything to do with the process of reading it. The basic message of television is television itself, the process, just as the basic message of a book is print. As McLuhan says, "The medium is the message."

This new view of our environment is much more realistic in the light of what has happened since the advent of McLuhan's "Electric Age." The Gutenberg Age, which preceded it, was one thing after another in orderly sequence from cause to effect. It reached its finest flower with the development of mechanical linkages: A acts on B which acts on C which acts on D on down to the end of the line and the finished product. The whole process was thus fragmented into a series of functions, and for each function there was a specialist. This methodology was not confined to making things; it pervaded our entire economic and social system. It still does, though we are in an age when cause and effect are becoming so nearly simultaneous as to make obsolete all our accustomed notions of chronological sequence and mechanical linkage. With the dawn of the Electric Age, time and speed themselves have become of negligible importance; just flip the switch. Instant speed.

However, our methodology and thought patterns are still, for the most part, based on the old fragmentation and specialism, which may account for some of our society's confusion, or perhaps a great deal of it.

Everybody talks about environment but nobody does anything about it. This is because, McLuhan says, "The moment a man recognizes his environment it becomes something else, his 'old environment,' and as such is the content of his new, or true, environment; which, of course, again is unseen."

Has he lost you already? Let's get out the bread crumbs: by "environment," he means that accustomed, unnoticed set of conditions which limits an organism's world at any given moment. In the ordinary course of events, we are not aware of our environment any more than a fish is aware of his. As Father John Culkin of Fordham, a leading McLuhanite, says, "We don't know who it was discovered water, but we're pretty sure it wasn't a fish."

Imagine a series of clear plastic domes, one within another. You can only see them from the outside; from the inside they are invisible. You become aware of an environment—one of these domes that surrounds you—only when you get outside of it. At that point you can see it. But you can't see the one which is *now* above you.

To put it another way, let us suppose that an ant has lived all his young life inside an anthill. He is not really aware that the anthill is his world; it simply *is* his world. So one day they send him off on his first important assignment, to drag back a dead beetle, say. He goes outside the anthill. Two things happen: 1) He sees the anthill for the first time; 2) He becomes aware that the world is a very big place. Does this mean that he is aware of his environment? No, because what he doesn't know is that his anthill is inside a greenhouse. The only way he'll become aware of the greenhouse is if he goes outside it. And even then it won't do him much good, because, you see, the greenhouse is inside the Houston Stadium, and so on. In each instance, you will notice that the old environment becomes content for the newer one, never the other way around. McLuhan, in one of his random conversational probes, notes that this seems to work out even in decor. Victorian furniture fits into a modern room, but a modern piece looks simply awful in a Victorian room.

So, awareness is becoming conscious that there is something higher controlling us than we had thought. The catch is that we can never catch up; we are always one step behind, for everything is contained by something bigger.

There are many sorts of environments besides the simple one of physical space which I mentioned: business, political, social, cultural, communications, etc. But for the moment let's just call it all environment. Two things will make us aware of an environment: either it changes or we do. A man who has lost a leg will become aware of steps. A man who has had five martinis may see things he has never seen before. A man who has had ten martinis may see things nobody has seen before.

There is another variety of environmental recognition reserved for those viewing it as outsiders. There are several varieties of what McLuhan calls "anti-environmentals," though I think "extra-environmental" is more descriptive.

An extra-environmental can be a person within a society whose perceptions have not been conditioned to obliviousness of the structure of a given environment. The story of the Emperor's new clothes is a good example. The child, because he was not yet committed to the environment power set-up, was not committed to see the Emperor's clothes, so he didn't. It was only when the extra-environmental child pointed out that he was naked that the others were able to see it too.

Similarly, a teen-ager and his other-conditioned perceptions will be extra-environmental in our Gutenbergish society.

A second type of extra-environmental is apparently due to an innate deficiency. That is to say that some people are unable to see things in a normal fashion.

On the other hand, they will see things that normal people can't. During the Second War, I understand that some aerial observers were recruited because they were colorblind. Their colorblindness made them unable to distinguish things designed for normal eyes, such as camouflage. They'd look down at a quite ordinary stretch of landscape and say, "Hey, there's a gun emplacement!" Because of their disability, their impairment of vision, their eyes were not taken in by the camouflage; all they could see was the thing itself. The extra-environmental thus has a great advantage, assuming he has anything else going for him. His mind isn't cluttered up with a lot of rules, policy, and other environmental impedimenta that often pass for experience. The more experience you have the less able you are to look at a given environment, especially your own, with fresh eyes.

I said earlier that one of the ways that we can become aware of environment is for it to change. However, sometimes an environment can change without our really noticing what has happened. Part of this is due to a lag in terminology, part to our Mechanical Age commitment to specialists.

Travel, as an example, has changed drastically, and I don't mean that it's just faster. Travel, for the most part, is no longer travel; it is a process which has a beginning and an end but virtually no middle. Travel is not an experience so much as a suspension of experience. Flying in a plane from San Francisco to New York is nothing more nor less than a horizontal elevator ride. One imagines that if we had buildings 3000 miles high, there would be a young woman on the elevators offering us coffee, tea, or milk.

Is terminology all that important? Yes, because to name things is to recognize them; it is the way we learn about our environment. Which brings us to specialism. The specialist is by nature environmental. If his environment changes he will not necessarily become extra-environmental. It is more likely that he will carry his tendency to specialism with him the way a snail does his shell. A born specialist will tend to interpret all experience in the light of his own expertise. *Illustrative story:* One time a cloak and suit manufacturer went to Rome and while he was there managed to get an audience with His Holiness. Upon his return a friend asked him, "What did the Pope look like?" The tailor answered, "A 41 Regular."

If specialism epitomizes the environmental stance, then "generalism" probably covers the extra-environmental. A generalist starts from the outside of a given environment; a specialist works on the inside. McLuhan has a special aversion to specialism; a sign in his office proclaims, "No specialist need apply." This does not mean that he is against professional expertise in the solution of problems, only against its built-in blinkers.

Once you take a problem to a specialist you are wired in to a specialist's solution. However well executed it is, the odds are against its being a real answer. Let us say that your company is having growing pains, and is uncomfortable in its present quarters. So you go to an architect. Let us also suppose that he is a very good architect, broad-thinking, one dedicated solidly to the proposition that form follows function. So he inquires after your needs, your ambitions, your hopes, your fears, what manner of people you are, etc. Do you know what you are going to end up with? A building. Now, a building, however nice, may not be the answer to your problem at all. Perhaps the real answer is to stop expanding, or fire the traffic manager, or everyone stay home and do cottage work connected by closed-circuit TV. But these are generalist solutions, not the sort of thing you expect

an architect to come up with. If he did, you'd probably think he was a busybody.

Those who find McLuhan most compatible are those who have already figured out a structure and wonder where it fits in the larger scheme of things. The generalist area looks like this, a circle:

The dot in the middle is you. The area within the circle is your field of specialization; therefore any problem solution (save one by a greater specialist) which fits inside will be unacceptable because you already know all about it, and have probably tried it, and it doesn't work. On the other hand, anything outside the circle is incomprehensible; any solution placed there will simply be inapplicable. The generalist problem-solving area has got to be right on the circumference itself: close enough in so that you get it, far enough out so that you can't pick it to pieces.

McLuhan's terminology accommodates this concept and improves it by expanding it into a process. He would call the inside of the circle "environment," and the outside "anti-environment." You can't really recognize things inside your environment, and you can't really see things outside it; so there we are sitting on the circumference again. The thing that is added by this change in terms is this: you solve problems by expanding the environmental area, by moving the circumference out.

McLuhan's most powerful appeal, in the end, is to those who have thought themselves into a sort of intellectual isolation, who lie awake and groan, "Doesn't anyone else think in the same patterns I do?" For some of these McLuhan does.

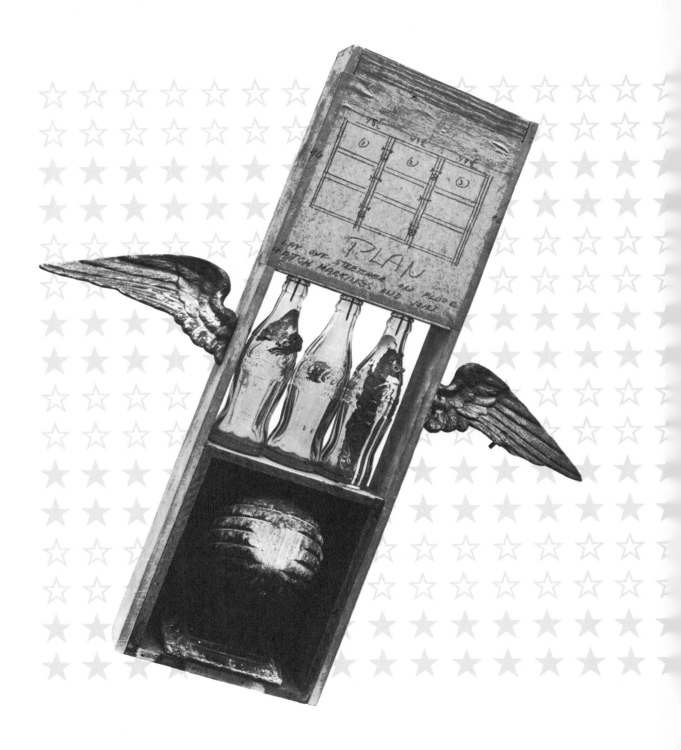

SUPPOSE HE IS WHAT HE SOUNDS LIKE, THE MOST IMPORTANT THINKER SINCE NEWTON, DARWIN, FREUD, EINSTEIN, AND PAVLOV —WHAT IF HE IS RIGHT?

TOM WOLFE

As McLuhan sees it—in the simplest terms, here is his theory step by step: People adapt to their environment, whatever it is, with a certain balance of the five senses: sight, hearing, touch, smell, and taste. If something steps up the intensity of one sense, hearing for example, the other senses will change intensity too, to try to regain a balance. A dentist, for example, can practically shut off pain—sense of touch—by putting earphones on a patient and pouring intense noise into his ear—sense of hearing.

Every major technology changes the balance of the senses. One of the most explosive of these technologies was the development of the printing press in the fifteenth century. Before that, people's senses still had pretty much the old tribal balance. That is to say, the sense of hearing was dominant. People got their information mainly by hearing it from other people. People who get their information that way are necessarily drawn closer together, in the tribal way. They have to be close to each other in order to get information. And they have to believe what people tell them, by and large, because that is the only kind of information they can get. They are interdependent.

They are also more emotional. The spoken word is more emotional than the written word. It carries emotion as well as meaning. The intonation can convey anger, sorrow, approval, panic, joy, sarcasm, and so forth. This *aural* man, the tribal man, reacts more emotionally to information. He is more easily upset by rumors. His and everybody else's emotions—a collective unconscious—lie very near the surface.

The printing press brought about a radical change. People began getting their information primarily by seeing it—the printed word. The visual sense became dominant. Print translates one sense—hearing, the spoken word—into another sense—sight, the printed word. Print also converts sounds into abstract symbols, the letters. Print is orderly progression of abstract, visual symbols. Print led to the habit of categorizing—putting everything in order, into categories, "jobs," "prices," "departments," "bureaus," "specialties." Print led, ultimately, to the creation of the modern economy, to bureaucracy, to the modern army, to nationalism itself.

People today think of print as if it were a technology that has been around forever. Actually, the widespread use of print is only about two hundred years old. Today new technologies—television, radio, the telephone, the computer—are causing another revolution. Print caused an "explosion"—breaking society up into categories. The electronic media, on the other hand, are causing an "implosion," forcing people back together in a tribal unity.

The aural sense is becoming dominant again. People are getting their information primarily by hearing it. They are literate, but their primary source is the radio, the telephone, the TV set. The radio and the telephone are obviously aural media, but so is television, in McLuhan's theory. The American TV picture has very low definition. It is

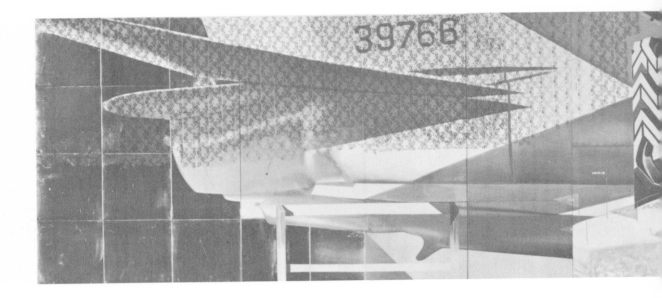

not three-dimensional, like a movie or a photo-graph, but two-dimensional, like a Japanese print or a cartoon. The viewer fills in the spaces and the contours with his mind, as he does with a cartoon. Therefore, the TV viewer is more *involved* in the TV image than in the movie image, he is so busy run-ning over the image with his eye, filling in this and that. He practically reaches out and *touches* it. He *participates;* and he likes that.

Studies of TV children—children of all social classes who are used to getting their information primarily by television—studies of this new genera-tion show that they do not focus on the whole pic-ture, the way literate adults do when they watch a movie. They scan the screen for details; their eyes run all over the screen, focusing on holsters, horses' heads, hats, all sorts of little things, even in the fiercest gun battles. They watch a TV show the way a non-literate African tribesman watches a movie—

But exactly! The TV children, a whole generation of Americans, the oldest ones are now twenty-five years old—they are the new tribesmen. They have tribal sensory balances. They have the tribal habit of responding emotionally to the spoken word, they are "hot," they want to participate, to *touch,* to be involved. On the one hand, they can be more easily swayed by things like demagoguery. The *visual* or *print* man is an individualist; he is "cooler," with built-in safeguards. He always has the feeling that no matter what anybody says, he can go check it out. The necessary information is filed away some-where, categorized. He can *look* it up. Even if it is something he can't *look* up and check out—for example, some rumor like "the Chinese are going to bomb us tomorrow"—his habit of mind is estab-lished. He has the feeling: All this can be investi-gated—*looked* into. The aural man is not so much of an individualist; he is more a part of the collec-tive consciousness; he *believes.*

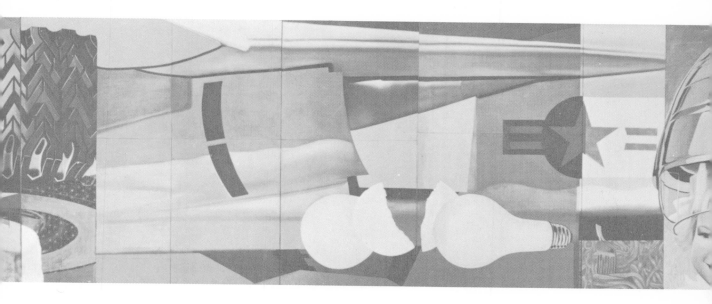

To the literate, visual, *print* man, that seems like a negative quality, but to the aural, tribal man, it seems natural and good. McLuhan is not interested in values, but if anything, he gives the worst of it to the literate man who is smug in the belief that his sensibility is the only proper one. The tribal man—the new TV generation—is far more apt at *pattern recognition,* which is the basis of computers. The child will learn a foreign language faster than a literate adult because he absorbs the whole pattern of the language, the intonations and the rhythms, as well as the meaning. The literate man is slowed down by the way he tries to convert the sounds to print in his mind and takes the words one by one, categorizing them and translating them in a plodding sequence.

In formal learning, in schools, that is, the new TV-tribal man is at a great disadvantage, however, given the current teaching methods. As McLuhan

sees it—if people think there is a bad drop-out problem in American schools today, it is nothing compared to what it is going to be like in another ten or fifteen years. There will be a whole nation of young psychic drop-outs—*out of it*—from the wealthy suburbs no less than the city slums. The thing is, all these TV-tribal children are *aural* people, *tactile* people, they're used to learning by pattern recognition. They go into classrooms, where they are taught by subjects, that is, categories: mathematics, history, geography, biology. It doesn't make *sense* to the tribal kids; it's like trying to study a flood by counting the trees going by; its *unnatural.*

It's the same way with these *cities* the *print*-minded rulers keep on piling up around them, *more* skyscrapers, *more* freeways pouring into them, *more* people piling into them. Cities are still based on the old idea of using space efficiently, of putting as many activities into a single swath of ground

as possible to make it easier for people to move around and do business with each other. To the new drop-out generation and the drop-out generations to come, this idea of lateral space and of moving people around in it doesn't seem very important. Even *visual* people have begun to lose a little of the old idea of space because of the airplane. When somebody gets on a jet in New York and flies to San Francisco in four hours, the time is so short, the idea of the space, the three thousand miles, loses its meaning. It is just like taking a "horizontal elevator," McLuhan says. In Los Angeles, with everybody traveling by car on freeways, nobody talks about "miles" anymore, they just say "that's four minutes from here," "that's twenty minutes from here," and so on. The actual straight-line distance doesn't matter. It may be faster to go by a curved route. All anybody cares about is the time.

For that matter—the drop-out generations will even get rid of the cars, says McLuhan. The car is

still largely tied to the idea of space, but the TV-tribal kids aren't. It even shows up in their dances. The new American dances, the twist, the frug, and all that, ignore the geography of the dance floor. The dancers stay in one place and create their own space. They jerk, spasm, hump, and bob around in one place with the sound turned up—aural! tribal!—up into the hot-jolly hyperaesthetic decibles. Eventually, says McLuhan, they will use the same sort of pattern in the way they work. They will work at home, connected to the corporation, the boss, not by roads or railroads, but by television. They will relay information by closed-circuit two-way TV and by computer systems. The great massive American rush-hour flow over all that asphalt surface, going to and from work every day, will be over. The hell with all that driving. Even shopping will be done via TV. All those grinding work-a-daddy cars will disappear. The only cars left will be playthings, sports cars. They'll be just like

horses are today, a *sport.* Somebody over at General Motors is saying—*What if he is right?*

STUDENT'S
GUIDE

The Role of the Mass Media

The Mass Media

Questions for Discussion

1. Which of the mass media have you come in contact with in the last week? Do you recall being affected by any one of them strongly, either positively or negatively? Do you recall gaining information that was particularly important to you from a mass medium? Which of the mass media do you think you generally have the most contact with?

2. Propaganda is usually defined as "the teaching spread by an organization or individual"; therefore, even though we may think of it as deceitful, propaganda can also have positive value. What examples of positive propaganda can you think of? What example of harmful propaganda does Stuart Chase give? Is it usually easy to tell the motives behind propaganda? Why, or why not?

3. What does Stuart Chase think is the primary danger of the mass media? What other cases do you know, besides the charges made by Joe McCarthy, of guilt by association being spread through the mass media?

4. What does the word "cybernetics" mean? What connection does it have with the mass media?

5. Read again what the author says at the end of page 11 about Art Buchwald's "Merry Christmas Wishes." What does "affluent" mean? In what ways does this poem illuminate our society?

Topics for Composition

1. Write your own "holiday message" to the American people. You may select an occasion other than Christmas, such as Thanksgiving, Independence Day, Veterans' Day, Mother's Day, or New Year's Day. If you wish, design a card to accompany your message.

2. In what ways did Senator Joe McCarthy use the mass media in the 1950s to get his message to the American people? How did his opponents use the media to make their opinions known? Do some research on McCarthy or another politician who used the mass media of his or her time, focusing your attention on ways in which the media played a part in that person's campaign. From your findings, prepare a paper to be shared with the class.

The Mass Media as "Languages"

Questions for Discussion

1. What specific examples might be used to support the idea, suggested in the first paragraph, that we don't see things as they fully are, as they really are? Is there any one idea or thing or person about which you know *all* there is to know? Is your ignorance your fault? Is it anyone's fault? Can we perceive anything except in relationship to ourselves?

2. A filter lets some things go through and keeps other things from going through. Are all filters the same? Do they keep what is bad away from you, as in smoking a cigarette, or do they sort out what is good for you, as in panning for gold? The author says that in the mass media, "filters play an invisible role in making us feel the way we do about a message." What does he mean by that?

Can you summarize the characteristics of each of the "language filters" that Roy Gallant discusses?

3. Read all the definitions of "medium" in an unabridged dictionary. See how many you can apply to one of the mass media—television, for instance. One definition says that a medium is a substance in which a specific organism lives and thrives. How is TV like that?

4. The author says, at the end of this article, "Language is a distinctively human activity." What does he mean by that? Can animals communicate a sense of past and future? Can they change their language? Can the media generate thoughts or only communicate them?

5. Pick a news event and tape record a television account of it. Then record a radio report of the same story, and collect a newspaper and a magazine account as well. Compare the various versions of the story. Does each medium change the story in some way? Does each one affect your feeling about the story differently? Share the different versions and your reactions to each of them with the class.

Topics for Composition

1. Why do you think the title of this book begins with the word "coping"? In what sense must mass media be coped with, or contended with? Do you feel that the mass media are "all around" us? Are they like people, in that we can choose to take or leave them? Or are they more like air, in that we cannot exclude them from our experience? Write your view (with examples) of coping with the mass media and keep this paper until you have finished studying this book.

2. Choose an event that happened recently in your school or community. Prepare an account of it in the inverted pyramid form, as if you were writing a story for a newspaper. Then write a magazine account of the same event. Try to include the same facts in each one.

The Mass Media— A Balance Sheet

Questions for Discussion

1. Do you agree with Stuart Chase that the media "insult your intelligence"? Which, if any, medium do you feel this about most frequently? Check through magazines and newspapers for ads that pander to the readers' "prejudices, appetites, and weaknesses." Bring a particularly clear example to class. Speculate on the motives of the ad's creators.

2. How would you answer the question asked by the author at the top of page 13? What could adults do to prevent young people from "dropping out"? Do schools give students "personal experience in influencing other people, or being influenced by them"? Why, or why not?

3. How would you interpret the painting on page 10? What does the white line mean to you? What might the partial word "OCO" represent? Is it some form of advertisement? What about the sign on the right?

Topics for Composition

1. Imagine that you live in a developing, third-world country. Your only image of the United States is from American movies and television, which you see occasionally. Describe the U.S. as you would expect to find it, based on your mass media experiences.

2. Stuart Chase describes the effect of the media coverage of the moon walk in 1968. Choose another more recent event and describe the effect that its media coverage had on you.

3. How many specific examples of the "assets" and "liabilities" in Chase's article can you find? Would you argue with any of these? Are there any assets which have now become liabilities, or vice versa?

As a class project, a large balance sheet might be created on a bulletin board, listing the assets (with examples) on one side and the liabilities (with examples) on the other. Make additions to Chase's list if you wish. Finally, write your own analysis of your mass media balance sheet.

Television

TV or Not TV

Questions for Discussion

1. The first two quotations imply that every aspect of television is educational. What different kinds of things have you learned from commercials, news, dramatic shows, variety shows, situation comedies, and documentaries? Do you sometimes learn from the ways people on TV dress? talk? solve problems? Do you think television has taught you to cope with any kinds of changes? If so, in what way?

2. After reading these comments, can you decide which ones criticize TV and which defend it? From your own personal opinions of TV, which points of view would you support? Why?

3. What is a "video cassette"? How might it bring the upheaval Mr. Youngblood predicts?

Topic for Composition

1. Choose one of the statements and write a short essay criticizing or defending it.

A Nation of Videots

Questions for Discussion

1. What does Jerzy Kosinski mean by a "videot"? Why would a "nation of videots" be for him "the ultimate future terror"? Would it be for you? Why?

2. What differences does Kosinski feel between reading a novel and watching TV? What are the differences in the two experiences for you? Do you always prefer TV to reading, or vice versa? Why?

3. Kosinski says that "the role television plays in our lives interests me very much." From your reading of his article, describe some aspects of that role as he sees it.

4. On page 23, Kosinski comments that "both young and old are acquiring via television, a superficial glimpse of a narrow slice of unreality." Describe some TV shows that might support this view and some that might not. Should TV have more "reality"? Why? In what ways?

5. Do you agree with Jerzy Kosinski that it is hard to judge the effect of TV in your life? Why? Which effects are you aware of? Do you think TV makes you observe people more and participate with them less?

6. Would you really prefer to watch a televised sport rather than attend the game yourself? Why? What about a parade? a riot? a political convention?

Topics for Composition

1. What are your very first memories of television? Think way back. Was it frightening? entertaining? funny? Write a story about a child's first encounter with TV. Perhaps it will be a mystery, perhaps a comic story. Use your imagination. Will the child be more interested in watching the show or in pulling the knobs off the set?

2. Are silence and an absence of entertainment threats to TV generations? to you? If so, do you think TV is a major cause? What about radio or film? Write about silence in your own life.

What TV Is Doing to America

Questions for Discussion

1. Judging by Alistair Cooke's first statement, as well as the rest of the interview, would you say that he sees television as harmful to our society? beneficial? both? Why do you think so? Would you expect him to agree with Jerzy Kosinski that "the word 'beneficial' doesn't apply to television. TV is simply a part of contemporary life. I must confront it, think about it, accept it, or reject it."? Why, or why not?

2. Do you think that people actually learn violence from television, or do they "get it out of their systems" by watching it on TV? Why do you think so? Does Alistair Cooke seem more concerned with violence in news coverage or in dramatic shows? Why?

3. What does Cooke mean by using television as "audible wallpaper"? Have you ever done that? Why, or why not? Do you think many people do? How, if at all, do you think the public's use of TV affects what shows get to be on television?

4. Cooke says that "in our country the primary function of television is that of a merchant." In what ways might TV be different if it were not a merchant? Would it be better or worse? Why?

5. What are the advantages of the British television system, as explained in this article? Can you think of any disadvantages? Do you watch both public and commercial TV? If so, what programs do you like and what do you dislike on each? Why?

6. "Television has exposed the whole mechanism of politics," says Cooke on page 31. Give examples to confirm or deny this statement. Is TV good or bad for politics, in your opinion?

7. What difference does Cooke feel that television makes in our attitudes toward war? In what ways can the freedom of our media work for us and against us?

8. Do you think TV commentators lack objectivity? What examples can you discuss? *Should* commentators try to be objective? Why, or why not?

9. What does Alistair Cooke mean by "genteel-

isms''? Compile a list of 20 of these (with translations) from television. For what different reasons do people use "genteelisms"? Are they ever justified? When are they harmful? Explain.

Topics for Composition

1. Pick an important story from today's newspaper and write a script for presentation on an evening news show for which you are anchorperson. (An important story runs up to three minutes.) Don't forget to indicate where you want to show film, maps, diagrams, interviews, etc. Will this be your lead item, or will you give other items top priority? Why?

2. What sort of program was Alistair Cooke's show, *Omnibus?* Do some investigating and report back to the class. Then reread what he says about it on page 30.

3. Reread the last three paragraphs of Cooke's statements. Describe in your own words what cynicism means, as it is used here. Can cynicism be either a good or a bad attitude? If so, in what ways can we tell the difference?

Violence on Television

Questions for Discussion

1. Have you often seen on television the type of violence pictured here? What other types of violence have you seen? Keep a record of your TV viewing for a week. How many programs did you watch? How many scenes of violence did you see?

2. How many of the four types of conflict mentioned on page 36 have you seen on television? Find examples of each of the four types in literature,

and bring them to class to discuss. What is the basic conflict? If it were dramatized, what kinds of sets and special effects would be necessary? How large a cast would be needed? After your discussion, would you agree with the comments on why the first three types are rarely shown on television?

How to Tell Good Guys from Bad Guys

Questions for Discussion

1. Is John Steinbeck's attitude toward television in this essay serious, humorous, or a combination of both? Point out specific places in the article to back up your opinion.

2. In Steinbeck's "digression" about Elia Kazan, a well-known theatrical director and writer, he makes the point that television advertising creates an artificial appearance in people. To what extent do you agree or disagree with him? By selling products and creating trends, TV can create patterns in dress and hairstyles. Do people conform in dress and looks more than they used to before television? less? about the same? Why?

3. Steinbeck points out some positive effects that TV has had upon his children. Do you think these are typical of the effects upon most children? Why, or why not? Can you think of similar positive effects that TV has had upon you?

4. Why do you think Steinbeck says that the Western is the "celebration of a whole pattern of American life that never existed"? What is *commedia dell' arte?* Why do you think Steinbeck relates it to the Western?

5. Do TV shows follow the predictable forms that Steinbeck's son describes? Summarize his de-

scription. Select a program that fits the general description and show how it fits. What other patterns can you find in TV Westerns, crime shows, or other TV dramatic programs?

6. What is your reaction to the final statement in this essay? Do you think the producer was criticizing the public? Why, or why not? If any group should be criticized, should it be the public or the TV producers? Why?

7. Steinbeck lists some Western heroes from past decades of movies, radio, and television. What are some traits of TV and movie Western heroes? Who were some of the more recent Western heroes? Are there any currently? Why?

Topics for Composition

1. Write a script for the scene which is shown on pages 36–37. What led up to this point? What is going to happen next? How do you know? Write *two* endings to your scene: one traditional and one a novel ending.

2. Imagine that you are a visitor to this planet from a distant galaxy, sent to observe the behavior of Earthlings. With your sophisticated equipment, you can tap into TV sets. Not only can you see what's on the set, you can see *through* the set and watch the people watching it. Describe an evening of watching both the programs and the audience in a home. Prepare this as part of a report to your native planet. What is this TV that Earthlings watch so much?

3. What differences are there between the historical Old West and the "Wild West" of TV Westerns? Steinbeck notes that clothing is one difference, for very practical reasons. Do some research and write a comparison of some aspect of the historical Old West with the TV version.

The "Swashbuckler" Movie

Questions for Discussion

1. Study the picture on page 42. Have you seen scenes similar to this in the movies or in old movies shown on TV? Who is the hero? the villain? How can you tell?

2. How would you define "hero"? Are there differences between the heroes you read about in books and those you see on television and in movies? What qualities do you feel a hero should have?

3. What do you think makes this script a cliché? Why would anyone bother writing a cliché? Why do you think such a story has audience appeal? To whom would it appeal most?

4. Do you think the makers of movies such as this want you to conclude that "the good, the true, and the beautiful" always win out over "the bad and the ugly"? Why, or why not? What are some of the differences between movies of this type and real life?

Topics for Composition

1. Look at the picture on page 45. The event on which this picture is based actually occurred in history. Do you suppose the actual event was as exciting and dramatic as that shown in the movie? Why, or why not? Write your own script for this movie scene.

2. Cut out two pictures from magazine ads or TV sections of newspapers. Write a short cliché script for each, similar to the ones in the book. Make sure to give each script a title, such as "The Soap Opera" or "The Soft-Sell Ad."

The "Political" Movie

Questions for Discussion

1. What is happening in the picture on page 46? on page 49? How many times have you seen pictures such as this in the movies? on television? in the news?

2. If all you knew about American politics was what you learned through pictures and movie scripts such as these, what conclusions would you draw concerning American politics and politicians? Would your conclusions be correct? Why, or why not? (Note, for example: The script indicates that the candidate had served time "on a chain gang," yet the public still wants him for governor. Has such a thing occurred in our history?)

3. Would you consider this type of movie to be propaganda? What is its "message"? What would be the danger of accepting the message as true?

Topic for Composition

1. Outline a cliché plot for a movie or TV drama about the 1976 election campaign. Then write the script for one scene within the story.

The "Society" Movie

Questions for Discussion

1. In a "society" movie, who is rich—the hero or the villain? How do you know?

2. Why do you think the feelings of the "poor boy" are shown to be more sincere than those of the high-society people? To what extent is propaganda involved in this situation? Is the hero rewarded in the end because poor people are always honest, they work harder, and their emotions are more sincere? What is "phony" about this view of American life? Why would people accept it?

3. Of movies or TV shows that you have seen recently, how many do you think are clichés? What kinds of propaganda do they put forth? How do they usually portray doctors, detectives, soldiers, teachers, hippies, lawyers, families? Do such portrayals have any effect on people's attitudes in real life? Why, or why not?

Topics for Composition

1. Summarize the plot of a clichéd TV show that you have seen recently. Suggest ways to change the plot to remove the clichés.

How to Talk Back to Your TV Set

Questions for Discussion

1. Nicholas Johnson would argue that treating television programming and values as necessary, inevitable, and our own, as if TV were a healthy appendage that we don't need to think about, is dangerous. After reading his argument, do you agree or disagree? Why? Had you ever considered the "myths" that he points out before reading this article? Do you think very many people are aware of such arguments? In what ways could they become more aware?

2. How does the amount of TV viewing in your home compare with the amounts given in the beginning of this article? Keep a record of your television watching for a week. How much time did you spend watching?

3. Why don't you watch certain shows? Are they

too stupid? too serious or intellectual? too much like other shows? What shows do you watch? Do you like them? Why?

4. Since TV signals are carried on public property—the air—should you be given more choice in programming? Do you think that the greatest percentage of audience should always determine what remains on the air? Why, or why not?

5. Suppose a method were developed to perfect pay TV. You could watch special programs or live events without commercials, but you would have to pay for the privilege at the end of the month, according to how many shows you watched. How would you react to this system? Do you think it would eventually wipe out free TV, or would free TV have to improve to coax viewers back? Would pay TV have some of the problems Nicholas Johnson finds in free TV? What ones might it have? Which would it not have?

6. TV news has been called a "headline service" which gives you brief impressions rather than full stories. It must be more selective than newspapers about which stories to cover because of time. If most citizens get their news entirely from TV, is this good or bad for democracy? Is "a little knowledge a dangerous thing"? Or is "some knowledge better than none at all"?

Topics for Composition

1. How do you feel about the picture on page 54? What do these details tell you about the person who is watching that TV: the location of the set, the darkness in the room, the blurry image on the screen? Describe being in this room.

2. If a sponsor objects to a certain scene in a program, should it have the power to remove that scene? Who should have that power? Write your specific suggestions in a letter to a network.

3. Who decides what shows get on the air? What is a "pilot film"? Who decides how long a show stays on the air? See what you can find out and report to the class.

Have the TV Networks Gone Too Far?

Questions for Discussion

1. In regard to Nicholas Johnson's forceful statement, *does* TV have an obligation to "help us understand the alternatives" to the kind of life it preaches? Or should it be entitled to do what it wants under the law of freedom of speech and the guise of business? What responsibility goes with any freedom?

2. What are the truths and limitations of Whitney Young's comment? How does his focus differ from Johnson's?

3. Frank Stanton says that the first evidence of political decay is "an effort to control the news media." Is it at all possible that political decay could *result from* a free but irresponsible news media? How?

TV Interviews

Questions for Discussion

1. Have you seen TV talk shows which illustrate the truth of Herbert Mitgang's comments? Do interviews on news or programs such as "Today" (NBC) illustrate them? Can you recall an example when an interviewer *did* dispute a half-lie or insert facts which seemed impolite? If so, describe it.

2. Look at the drawing by Saul Steinberg on page 64. Why is the TV set drawn as a seductive woman? In what ways can television seduce?

Radio

Radio, the Parent Reborn

Questions for Discussion

1. How would you describe radio, as you usually think of it? Do you really listen to it? Does it simply keep you company? Do you turn it on for specific programs? Do you agree or disagree with Les Brown's description, "a medium much taken for granted and usually connected in our minds with recordings and chatter"? Why?

2. What characteristics of radio does Les Brown specify as being valuable in emergency situations? Which of these does television lack? Has radio ever helped you in an emergency, as it did for Les Brown during the 1965 power blackout in New York?

3. Have you ever listened to replays of old radio dramas, such as "The Shadow," "The Lone Ranger," "Inner Sanctum," or comedies, such as "Jack Benny," "Fibber McGee and Molly," or "My Little Margie"? Did you enjoy the "theater of the mind"? Why? Do you think you could enjoy it as much as or more than television? Why, or why not? Would you like to be able to "see" more radio than you can in current programming?

4. What is your favorite radio station? your second favorite? What are your parents' favorite stations? Why do you prefer your station? How often do you listen to it? How does that compare with your parents' listening patterns? Does your timetable of listening fit with the one Les Brown describes, or is it different? You may want to put these answers onto a chart for the whole class, in order to compare the amounts and kinds of radio use.

5. According to the author, "The theory in radio today is that regular listeners want the station to be the same all the time," and thus, most stations have specialized in a "rigid format." Do you like stations to be specialized? Why? Do you ever find a station *too* predictable? Would you like to see television follow the "rigid format" theory? How do you think that would affect the quality of progamming?

6. What does this article tell you about the difference between the station-network relationships in radio and in television? Do you think that has anything to do with the possibility of eliminating government regulation of radio? Why is such a move not being considered for television?

7. What is the real difference between FM and AM broadcasting methods? Why is the range of each different?

Topics for Composition

1. The author asks three questions on page 71. What is your answer to each of them? Write a letter to the Federal Communications Commission in support of your views.

2. Specialized frequencies outside the regular broadcast bands serve police, fire, ship-to-shore, and other uses. Prepare a list of the specialized uses of radio and share it with the class.

3. Compile a list of all the radio stations in your city (or the nearest large city, if you live in a small town). Find out the format of each station—top 40, country and western music, foreign-language programming, news, etc. Which station has the largest audience? (Any advertising agency can give you that information.)

4. If you have access to a tape recorder, try some experimenting with sound effects, using common household items such as a balloon, cellophane, or a cookie sheet. See if you can create the sounds of a storm (thunder, wind, rain), footsteps, and a squeaky door opening and closing. What other sounds can you simulate? Remember that just a few words can identify and add to the effectiveness of your sound effects. Even a brief line such as, ''Those clouds are gathering fast,'' will make the difference between hearing a shaking cookie sheet and hearing thunder.

As you become familiar with the possibilities of sound effects, try writing a short scene for the theatre of the mind. It needn't be too elaborate: a brief dialogue or even a monologue backed by sound effects can suggest that you are broadcasting from a setting such as a stormy beach, a crowded street corner, or a cozy fireside. Produce your radio script on tape for the class.

5. What are some of the identifying features of various radio stations in your area, other than their call letters? Record a short segment from five radio stations. Play the segments in class to see whether everybody can name the station from some identifying point, such as a bit of a news program or a short segment of an announcer's voice. If you had your own station, what would be its format and features? Describe or outline its programming for a week, the type(s) of announcers it would have, whether it would have a rigid format or not, etc.

Newspapers

Finding Your Way through the Newspaper

Questions for Discussion

1. Obtain at least two different newspapers, or more than one edition of the same paper. Use a crayon or felt-tip pen to mark each of the parts of a front page listed in the article. Which of the parts listed do they *not* contain? How are the sections of the papers identified? How are the newspapers numbered?

2. Create your own front-page layout. Cut out headlines and stories from three different newspapers. Using a piece of newspaper as a backing, lay the materials out according to the specifications you've learned for a front page. Lengthen some articles, if you wish, by including additional material from other pages. If necessary, shorten articles written in inverted pyramid form. When you are finished, glue or tape the layout to the backing. Finally, compare your layout to others in the class and discuss the procedures and problems involved in laying out a front page.

Working Newsman Reveals How Newspapers Are Put Together

Questions for Discussion

1. What was your reaction to this article? Had you ever considered how complicated it is to put out a newspaper? Which things were the most surprising to learn about newspaper publishing? the most disturbing? Why? Do you think the author writes as an "insider" from the newspaper business? What clues can you find to that effect in the article?

2. On page 85, the author says, "On almost all papers the advertising department determines total pages to be printed and only after this does news receive its allocation." Why is this decision left to the advertising department rather than the news department? Which is more important to the reader—the news or the advertising? to the newspaper? Why?

3. On page 86, the author discusses several mechanical methods of printing. After reading his description, can you decide which method is pictured on page 82? What is the man doing?

4. Would you like to be a "gatekeeper"? Specifically, why, or why not? The author tells us: "One very fast gatekeeper took an average of four seconds to handle . . . a story of 225 words." How long does it take you to read that number of words? Do you think that instant decisions to drop or expand stories are a necessary disadvantage of the newspaper medium? Why, or why not?

5. What types of stories would you expect to appeal to a gatekeeper? If you were a journalist, how would you try to see that your story got past the gatekeeper? In what way does the inverted pyramid help the gatekeeper's job?

6. Although "official news policy is usually vague," certain newspapers are characterized as "liberal" or "conservative." Study the editorial pages of at least two newspapers (perhaps one you read and one your parents read). From the types of material included and the "slant" of the articles, what, if any, conclusions can you draw about the editorial policy of each newspaper? Can you find any evidence of "policy" or "slant" elsewhere in the newspapers? What are some examples?

7. Suppose that news technology became as advanced as the author describes in the last few paragraphs of his article. What types of stories would you want to see more of? What type would you call for least? Why?

Topics for Composition

1. Collect a newspaper for one week. Make a chart showing the amount of news, features, opinion, and advertising on each day. Express the amounts in *column inches:* use a ruler or yardstick to measure the length of the articles in inches, excluding headline space. (If the article is set on a column twice as wide as the others, don't forget to multiply your measurement by two.) Write a brief interpretation of your findings.

2. Try to obtain various newspapers to get different accounts of a similar story. Perhaps you can collect several big city papers, *The Wall Street Journal,* a local newspaper, a weekly tabloid, and possibly even a foreign paper. Cut out the articles (with headlines) and mount them. Write a comparison of the different versions: Which newspaper seemed closest to the "original wire service" article? How do the versions differ in length? in the amount of information included? in the kind of information given? in "slant"? in tone?

Humor in the Headlines

Topics for Composition

1. Have you ever run across headlines like these when reading the newspapers? Do you think any of these were intentionally done? Why, or why not? Can you decide what is wrong in each of them? Rewrite any 12 of them so that they say what they were actually meant to say.

2. Choose one headline in this article that interests you most. Assume that what it says is actually true and compose a news story to go along with it.

3. Can you find in newspapers you read other examples of such headlines? of interesting typographical errors? of unintentional or ironic humor within news stories? Try keeping a scrapbook of these examples during the rest of the course.

Interpreting the News

Questions for Discussion

1. How do you react to these interpretations? Do you find them amusing? cynical? truthful? Which ones do you appreciate most? Why? Have you actually heard these phrases and made these interpretations yourself? Which phrases have you heard most often?

2. For what specific reasons do you think the phrases listed under "What They Say" are used in reporting the news? Does this type of wording protect the people who are in the news? the people reporting the news? Do you think this type of wording can do any harm? Why, or why not?

Topics for Composition

1. Can you find any similar phrases to those under "What They Say" from the newspapers and from TV or radio news? You might add the phrases, and your own interpretations, to another part of the scrapbook you started for "Humor in the Headlines."

Statements

Questions for Discussion

1. What is your response to the remarks by the Midwestern Editor on page 101? What kind of news do you really enjoy reading? Why? Is there any news that you feel is necessary although you may not enjoy reading it? If so, what kinds? What purposes do you think a newspaper should fulfill?

2. In response to the statement on page 101, have you ever thought of fiction as "one lie after another"? What, if anything, is the difference between lies and fiction? In what way, specifically, could a journalist tell a lie with a series of truths? How does this question relate to the phrases under "Interpreting the News"? to the statement by Thomas Jefferson on page 101?

Advertising

Advertising through the Mass Media

Questions for Discussion

1. Which of the quotations at the start of this article comes closest to your usual feeling about advertising? If neither one expresses it, what is your feeling?

2. What does "meretricious" mean? Why do you think Jeremy Tunstall used that word in his statement on page 105? What feeling is he trying to communicate?

3. Briefly list 15 advertising messages which have reached you in the last week (the product's or service's name and a portion or description of the ad will be enough). Which ones have stayed in your mind the most? After each item, try to list where you received the message (TV, radio, billboard, magazine, etc.). Underline with one line any of the products you might like to try. Use two lines to underline any product you already use. Place an X after any product you would never use. Compare your list with those of other class members: Are there many duplications? What is the total number of different ads represented? How many advertising messages would you estimate that you normally encounter in a day, including billboards, signs and displays outside and inside stores, radio and TV messages?

Topic for Composition

1. What do you think are the qualities of good advertising? What should an ad accomplish? What should it not do? Why? Have you ever seen or heard a good advertisement? Can you recall what made you think so? Write a definition of good advertising and share it with the class. Then save it for use later in this chapter.

Understanding the Ads

Questions for Discussion

1. Have you recently bought an item that was labelled with any of the "special vocabulary" given on pages 110 and 111? Did the sale price really entice you? Did you later feel disappointed in your purchase? Why, or why not?

2. What other phrases in printed advertising, besides those given on pages 110 and 111, have you learned to mistrust or interpret? Why?

3. Have you ever seen informative advertising that was not in a mail-order catalog? If so, where? For what products or services would you like to have informative advertising?

4. Would you classify most of the ads you see on television as product differentiation or as informative advertising? Why do you think that is so? Do you think television is a medium that is better suited for the one kind of advertising than the other, or is the prevalence of one kind just an arbitrary choice by the advertisers? Why? Are magazines better suited for the one kind than the other? If so, in what ways?

5. Cut out several examples of product-differentiation ads which refer to the same type of product. Next to each one, write the reason that the advertiser wants you to buy that product rather than

another. Circle any "special vocabulary" in each ad. Do you find any differences? If so, what are they? Are there any actual "bargains" among them? Why?

Topics for Composition

1. Go to a large chain supermarket. Select a product such as breakfast cereal and examine the prices. List five members of the product-family you've chosen, along with the supposed advantage of each ("100% natural cereal" or "the laxative cereal"). Try to include both national and store brands. Record the price and net weight of each size package of each of the five brands. Also include the first four ingredients on the label. (By law, ingredients must be listed in the order of concentration in the product.) Using your findings, make a chart of the price-per-ounce (or other units) of the products and their ingredients. What, if any, is the "best buy" among the products? Why?

2. The authors mention in their discussion of "list price" that a few items are "fair traded" or price-fixed. Do some research on "fair trade laws." What exactly are they? When were they started? Why were they legislated in the first place? Whom did they benefit? Were they a good idea? Present your research as a lecture or an essay.

Four Ads for Discussion

Questions for Discussion

1. Did you like reading and looking at these advertisements? Which one did you like best? Why?

2. It's easy to find the "message" in each of the advertisements—the designer has crystallized it at the bottom of the page, near the sponsor's name. Why do you think each one was placed there?

3. What do you notice about the sentence structure in these ads? Are most of the sentences long or short? What about the paragraphs? Are there any sentence fragments? Where? Why do you think this kind of structure is used? In what way is it effective?

4. The tone of most advertising language is very direct, and first and second person pronouns often appear. Why is that? What is the effect created by sentences such as, "Come back to your senses," "We want you to live," or "If you don't do it, it won't get done"?

5. What, specifically, is the appeal of each of these ads? How do the advertisers who created each message want you to feel: sensual? cared about? fearful? concerned? guilty? What specific things did each advertiser do to bring about those responses? Look again at the design and the copy of each ad. Did you feel what the advertiser set out to make you feel? Why?

6. Do these ads call upon your reason at all? Summarize in one or two sentences the "argument" of each. Which of these ads is the most informative? What information is conveyed? What else, if anything, would you like to know from the ad, other than the information given?

7. What other kinds of emotional appeals have you experienced in advertising? Find at least two examples of ads with appeals different from the ones in this book, mount them on paper or cardboard, and bring them to class. See whether the class agrees with your analysis of the ad's primary appeal, as well as any secondary appeals that might be present. Point out the factual information, or lack of it, in each ad.

8. There has been a good deal written and said on the subject of emotional appeal in advertising, much of the comment very critical. What is your view of advertising's use of emotional appeal? Is

there anything wrong with using it? Do some appeals seem more acceptable or ethical than others? Why, or why not? Give specific examples. Would you like to have all advertising be strictly informative, without any appeal to the emotions or senses? Why, or why not? What, specifically, is the value of being aware of emotional appeal in advertising?

9. Check back to your earlier definition of good advertising. Do any of the four ads in the book fulfill your standards? Do you find their use of emotional appeal acceptable? Why, or why not? What do you think are the best qualities of each of these ads?

Topics for Composition

1. Look for an ad in which the appeal has little or no reasonable connection with the product or service. A toothpaste which promises sex appeal would be one example. Describe your reaction to that ad and suggest reasons why the advertiser chose that approach. Then describe a new approach which you would prefer.

2. Collect as a class some technical, business, and religious magazines, as well as an assortment of popular magazines on sports, news, beauty, etc. Which magazines have the most informative advertising? Which have the most emotional? beautiful? well-reasoned? Choose any two of the magazines and discuss what you can tell about the audience for those magazines from looking at their ads.

3. Medical doctors are inundated by advertisements from drug companies who are eager to have them prescribe their brand of drug by its trade name, rather than a possibly equivalent and less expensive drug under its generic name. One technique the drug companies use is creating easy-to-remember trade names and tongue-twist-

ing generic names for the same drug: compare Darvon with propoxyphene hydrochloride, or Vasodilan with isoxsuprine hydrochloride.

Obtain ten drug ads from your family doctor, who will undoubtedly have plenty to give you. Analyze each ad. How do the advertising techniques differ from those of medical ads aimed at a mass audience of consumers?

Feature-by-Feature Advertising

Questions for Discussion

1. Describe some "feature-by-feature" ads that you have seen. Does this approach usually appear more often in magazines or on television? Can you think of any reason why?

2. What types of claims did you find in these ads? What is a "Dynamic Speaker"? What is "Slide Rule Vernier Tuning"? Have you ever seen an "inconvenient" carrying handle? Would you expect the pages on a memo pad to be "unmatched"?

3. Why, specifically, do you think advertisers use feature-by-feature advertising? Might it be used in honest, informative advertising? In what specific ways could it be used helpfully?

Topics for Composition

1. Collect examples of feature-by-feature advertising. Which ones seem honest and informative? Which ones seem full of suspect claims? Write down examples of each kind and explain how you decided which ones were more believable than others. (Note: Colleges and military recruiters often use this technique in their brochures.)

2. Prepare an ad for any product or service you wish, using feature-by-feature advertising well. Mount the finished ad for display.

Can Advertisers Back Up Their Claims?

Questions for Discussion

1. Have you heard or read performance claims such as those listed in the article? If so, list as many as you can and discuss them with the class. Did you believe these claims? Do you question them now? Why, or why not?

2. What products, other than those in the article, habitually use performance claims? Name five if you can. Why do you think that manufacturers of these products rely heavily on this advertising approach?

3. From your reading of this article, would you say that the largest problem in the claims cited is with dishonest or with useless information? Is there a difference? Is it honest for an advertiser to base a performance claim on irrelevant data? Why, or why not? Of all the results that are given here, which one(s) seem to you to be the worst advertising? Why?

4. Do you think the Federal Trade Commission's method of protecting consumers is effective? Should government "keep its nose out" of private industry? Why, or why not? If you support the FTC's approach, as outlined in this article, what do you think should be done with advertisers whose performance claims are found to be un-supported? Should they be fined? jailed? forced to print a retraction?

Topics for Composition

1. In what ways can consumers check on advertising claims? Do you know what publications and organizations are available for consumers? If not, do some investigating of national and local groups which answer various kinds of consumer problems and report your findings to the class.

2. Obtain an issue of *Consumer Reports, Changing Times,* or another magazine which evaluates products and services. Read their evaluation of a particular item. Then collect ads for that item and compare them to the nonbiased information. What can you conclude? Present your findings in a written report which tells your sources and includes the ads.

3. Advertisers conceivably could print fantastic, dishonest performance claims, publish their ads nationwide, and then agree to withdraw the ads after many people have seen them. As one way to prevent this, Congress could pass a law requiring advertisers to submit their ads to a commission before publishing them. Would you support this idea? Why, or why not? If not, would you support a similar law that covered only certain products, such as drugs? What would be the consequences of such a law? What does the legal concept of "prior restraint" mean, and how would it apply to this situation?

Prepare your answer in the form of a letter which you might send to your Congressperson if such a law were proposed. (Include the correct name and address of your Representative.)

Advertising Portraying or Directed to Women

Questions for Discussion

1. Earlier in this book, you discussed the influence of the mass media upon your thinking and your life. Do you think that the advertisers who prepared this report believe that advertising merely reflects behavior in society or also influences it? Why?

2. What were your reactions to this article? Were you encouraged by it? surprised? skeptical? angered? Have you ever seen examples of the types of advertising discussed in it? If so, describe specific ads and your reactions to them.

3. The National Advertising Review Board is made up of people within the advertising business. Does it surprise you that they would issue a statement such as this? Why, or why not? Would the article have been any different if it had been written by a women's rights group? If so, in what ways?

4. Watch television for two hours. Make your own survey of the commercials you see, similar to the survey discussed on pages 126–127. Do your results differ from those given in the article? If so, in what ways? Are there any ads which have recently changed their portrayals of women or of families, but which you still find objectionable? If so, why?

5. Do you think there is other discrimination in advertising, besides that directed toward women? Are stereotyped characters ever a form of discrimination? If so, in what way? What are some stereotypes of men which are communicated in advertising? Can advertising exist without stereotypes? Why, or why not?

Topics for Composition

1. Collect two ads which violate the recommendations in this article and two which fulfill them. Explain in two or three sentences for each one how you reached your conclusion.

2. What were the advertising world's portrayals of and approaches to women prior to the 1970s? Select a decade between 1920 and 1970 and investigate old magazines or books of old advertisements from that period. What kinds of messages were directed to women? What were women in ads like? Drawing upon your findings, write a comparison between the role of women in the ads of the particular decade you have investigated and in advertising today.

3. "What sort of man reads *Playboy*?", a feature appearing in many issues of that magazine, noted the spending habits and interests of readers for the benefit of readers and advertisers both. Select a magazine or TV show which appeals to one segment of the mass public and prepare your own feature entitled, "What sort of person reads (or watches)——————?" Be satirical if you want to, but use your actual impressions of the audience as if you were giving this opinion to an advertiser.

4. Try to obtain a copy of a publication for advertisers, such as *Advertising Age,* and read it. What do advertising people write about for each other? Was it what you expected? Write a summary of what you found in the magazine.

Nothing Personal

Questions for Discussion

1. Have you ever flicked through the channels just to watch the commercials? Was your experience

like James Baldwin's? Why, or why not?

2. There are only four sentences in this piece. Why do you suppose Baldwin chose to make that third sentence so long? What feeling did you have when you read it?

3. Some entertainers, such as George Carlin, Stan Freberg, or the Firesign Theater, have used TV commercials as comedy material. Why are TV commercials so funny? Why do people laugh at them?

4. What is Baldwin saying here about the effects of TV commercials upon viewers? Do you think he would agree with Nicholas Johnson that "every minute of television programming . . . teaches us something"? Why do you think he uses the words "defeated," "forbidden," "prevented," and "subversive" in the description? What is he saying about the relationship of our fears to advertising? How would you interpret the last line of this passage?

Topic for Composition

1. As a researcher for a distant planet, you are assigned to prepare a list of American desires, cares, and concerns as illustrated by their TV commercials that you intercept. Prepare a specific report of your viewing for your commander. What are these people like? What gifts might they appreciate? Are they intelligent beings?

Movies

The Camera and the Audience

Questions for Discussion

1. Gilbert Seldes talks primarily about the technique of movies in this article. Have you been aware very often of the "process" behind a film or a TV show? Do you watch to see *what* happens, or *how* it happens, or both? What are some advantages and disadvantages of becoming aware of how movies are made?

2. Do you think, from reading this article, that Seldes was an enthusiastic movie-goer? If so, which of his statements tell you so? Is there anything about his style that conveys this strong feeling? Explain.

3. Seldes makes the point that "the way movies tell their stories satisfies us as much as the stories they tell." Do you agree or disagree with this statement? Why? Do other media—comic books, for instance—qualify for this distinction as well? If so, which ones? Why?

4. On page 136 the author says, "The annihilation of ordinary time is one of the most extraordinary effects the movies can produce." Have you ever seen a movie that made you lose all sense of

time? Can you recall any one way that effect was produced? Describe that film or part of it.

5. What does Seldes mean when he says, "There is no 'meanwhile' in the movies"?

6. Describe a scene which affected you strongly from a movie that you have seen recently. How did the director use long shots, medium shots, and closeups to control your attention? How were dialogue and music handled in the scene?

7. Gilbert Seldes wrote this piece in the mid-1950s. Do you think that the prediction he makes in the final paragraph has come true? What movies have you seen which are highly imaginative and dreamlike? What recent films have used "(newsreel) facts"? Have you seen any film in which it was especially hard to separate imagination from reality? If so, try to describe it.

Topics for Composition

1. Agree as a class to watch a specific movie on TV, or view a rented film together. Keeping this article in mind, make brief notes while watching about the order and length of specific shots or scenes, and be prepared to discuss them. (Use LS, MS, and CU to abbreviate long shot, medium shot, and closeup.)

2. Work individually or in groups on a movie timetable. Using a film history, such as Arthur Knight's *The Liveliest Art* (New American Library) or Gerald Mast's *A Short History of the Movies* (Pegasus paperback, The Bobbs-Merrill Co.), discover when movies were invented. When were D. W. Griffith's films made? What are his most famous works? When were cartoons first filmed? When did sound come in? And so forth. Post the timetable where you can refer to it during this chapter's study.

3. Seldes explains how filmmakers use the camera "to prevent us from seeing too much." Write a script in which you describe each shot for a short silent sequence which uses the camera to prevent the audience from seeing too much. If you have access to a movie camera, film your script once it has been approved.

The New Movies

Questions for Discussion

1. This article talks about a "younger" audience having emerged for movies. List all of the movies mentioned in the article. Put a check after each one you have seen, a plus after each one your parents have seen, and a check-plus after each one both you and they have seen. Compare your results with those of others in the class. What can you say about viewing patterns in the two generations?

2. Do you go to "the movies" or to "a movie"? In what ways do you decide which movie you will go to see? Do your parents decide in the same way?

3. What are your favorite movies? Why? What is it that makes one film experience better than another for you? What films have you seen lately? How did you react to them? Why?

4. According to this article, what are the characteristics of the "new" movies? Are they new in technique? audience? values? characters? Are theme and director as important, if not more so, than the starring actors? List as many film directors as you can. Which ones' films have you actually seen?

5. Why do you think people today prefer actors that they can identify with? In what specific ways have the heroes in our movies changed? Have they

disappeared? What, if anything, do your answers tell you about changes in our society?

6. This article names a number of currently successful actors. What names of female stars can you add to this list? How would you describe the image or images of women in American films at present? Would you like to see that image change? If so, in what ways?

Topics for Composition

1. Cut out ads for movies from the movie section of a big city newspaper. Label each major ad with the age group you think the film primarily appeals to. Collect ads in the same way twice more in the next two weeks. What can you say about the different segments of the movie audience today?

2. Write a review of a recent film that you have seen, discussing it in terms of the characteristics of the "new" movies given in this article. For example, did it involve "the search for a better way of life"? If so, in what ways? If not, what seemed to be its purpose? What were the major characters like? Did their identities seem larger or smaller than the theme of the movie? Be as specific as you can without "giving it away" to those who haven't seen it.

The Future of Hollywood

Questions for Discussion

1. According to this article, in what ways has the movie industry gradually turned television from a threat to a source of profit?

2. What do you predict for the future of movies—big money films? small, low-budget films? both? Why?

Topic for Composition

1. Conduct a survey among your parents and friends. What would they think about pay TV giving them the option of seeing movies right in their own home? Summarize the results of the survey and give your own opinion.

Hollywood's Mavericks

Questions for Discussion

1. What exactly does "maverick" mean? Where did the word originate? What are its positive and negative connotations?

2. Which films mentioned in his article does author Hollis Alpert consider to be "system" films? List them. Then list those which resulted from the "maverick method." Put a star after each movie that you have seen and compare your list with those of others in the class. Are you a "system" or "maverick" group?

3. What are some of the actual differences between "system" and "non-system" films? List and discuss as many as you can from this article and from your experience as a movie-goer.

4. Do you think, as director Paul Mazursky suggests on page 151, that some movies cause "the level of taste" to be lowered? What does he mean, specifically, by that? Can movies raise the public's tastes? Can you think of an example?

5. On page 153, John Cassavetes says that certain creative people in Hollywood "regard their main job as expressing their version of what life is and what people are feeling." Is that what you go to movies to see? Do some people go to movies to *escape* this? Should there be movies to fit both these needs? Why, or why not?

6. Alpert tells us that the management which produced *Towering Inferno* and *Airport 1975* in response to the financial successes of *The Poseidon Adventure* and *Airport* argue that they are "giving the public what it obviously wants." Do you agree or disagree? In what ways, if at all, does this argument differ from that of the TV broadcasters who are discussed by Nicholas Johnson on pages 56–57 of this book?

7. Do you agree or disagree with the last sentence in this article? Why?

Topics for Composition

1. What are the responsibilities of a director? What does a producer do? a distributor? an exhibitor? a screenwriter? an editor? See what you can find out about any one of these jobs, write down the information, and compile a class report on behind-the-screen work in the movie industry.

2. You are an independent, young director who has a brilliant, original idea for a new movie. Write a proposal to a studio that you want to bankroll the film. The proposal should describe the film's idea, who will star in it, the type of audience who will go to see it, and the reason your film will be different from any film yet made.

3. You are a producer for a large studio who wants to do a movie which is based on past successes and is sure to be "good box office." Write a letter to a director of your choice offering him the opportunity to work on this picture. Your letter should explain the movie's idea, stars, potential audience, and why it is sure to be a success.

Reel One

Topic for Composition

1. What movie might the narrator in this poem have seen? Why do you think he says "there wasn't much blue in the drifts or corners"? Think about a movie you have seen that was "like life, but better." Describe what the world outside the theater was like when you came out of the movie.

Trash, Art, and the Movies

Questions for Discussion

1. In her article, film critic Pauline Kael describes many things she likes and dislikes about specific movies and types of movies. What is the last movie you saw? Discuss some things in the movie you liked and some you disliked. If you have a favorite *type* of movie, what is it?

2. Does more than one person have to agree on the "good" things in a movie before they are really good? Do you always make your judgments about films, or is your judgment already made for you? If so, by whom? to what degree? Do you ever feel there are certain "official" responses that are right or wrong? Why, or why not?

3. Pauline Kael comments on page 161 that "so many people fall for whatever is talked about that they make the advertisers' lies true." Do you agree or disagree? Why? To what other mass media might this statement apply? In what way?

4. How would you describe Pauline Kael's writing style? Does she seem to speak directly to you? Does she make you believe in her love for

movies? If so, how? What general statement can you make about her view of movies?

5. What are some really good crime movies? What do you expect in a good crime movie? Do you usually get what you expect? What makes the difference? Do you think violence is stronger when it is acted out in front of you, or when it is only suggested? Give examples from films you have seen.

6. How fast can you describe the plot of an old-fashioned cowboys-and-Indians movie? Would it take longer to describe a more recent Western? In what ways have portrayals of both cowboys and Indians changed just since *High Noon* was made in 1952?

7. When you were a child, what types of movies did you see? Which ones did you like? Why? Were you frightened by them? upset in other ways? Should children's movies include pain, death, sorrow, punishment? Why, or why not?

Topics for Composition

1. Describe specifically a "little thing" that you particularly liked in a film.

2. Collect reviews by two other film critics from newspapers or books. Compare these to Pauline Kael's article: Do they talk about specific "little things" in the movie or about broad themes and trends? Do the writers seem to be talking to you or to someone else? Why? Are the styles of writing widely different, or do they seem much the same? In what ways?

   After studying these reviews, put them aside and recall a movie which is still vivid in your mind. Or if you can, go out and see one. Then write a review in which you describe your ideas and feelings about it.

Have the Movies Gone Too Far?

Questions for Discussion

1. Against what argument is Judith Crist defending the movies? What have they been accused of? What purpose is served by the example of the "ad for a plain, old-fashioned shoe sale"?

2. What is your reaction to the Swedish rating system, as it is illustrated in the passage here? Do you agree or disagree with the Swedes' attitudes toward violence in movies? toward sex in movies?

3. What, if any, relationship would Bergen Evans see between American violence among young people and American movies? Do you think excessive violence in films is dangerous? Is it dangerous for all viewers? Why, or why not?

4. Who should decide how much violence or sex is shown in movies? the film maker? local authorities? a national board?

5. What would you expect Jack Valenti's view to be on these topics: censorship; total freedom for film makers; the job of film critics; the responsibility of parents to children? Do you think you should be allowed to see any film? Should someone two years younger? four years younger? six years younger? Explain your answers.

Topic for Composition

1. The First Amendment to the U.S. Constitution guarantees that "Congress shall make no law . . . abridging the freedom of speech . . ." Are movies protected speech under the First Amendment?

   Prepare a research paper on the history of movie censorship in the United States. This is a big project if you want to do it thoroughly, but it can be broken down for several people to work on parts of it. Some can find out about freedom of speech and First Amendment law; others, the development of the Motion Picture Code; private censorship bodies, such as the National Catholic Office of Motion Pictures (formerly the Legion of Decency); the current rating system (G, GP, R, X); and finally, attitudes on censorship in your own community. Compile the information into a report which includes a thesis about movie censorship in this country.

A New Understanding of Media

The New Languages

Questions for Discussion

1. If you're not familiar with Marshall McLuhan's thought and style of writing, a first exposure can be unsettling. Traditional paragraphs do not exist. There is a plan, but within its parts, generalizations are not always developed. The separate thoughts must be absorbed one at a time. What was your reaction to this article as you read it? Do you think this disconnected, disorderly style is necessary to make the point about this being a non-linear, non-paragraph age? Or does the author simply need to work a little harder on his style?

2. Does the typographical design of this selection look like a unified body of paragraphs? Why, or why not? Did you notice the "new" visual language of the numbers in the margins? How did you react to them?

3. What is "frozen language"? Does the increase over the years in the size of dictionaries give evidence that language can't be frozen? Why, or why not? What is "lineal expression"? What does the author mean by "multi-perspective"?

4. What does it mean to say that a newspaper reader is thrown into a "producer role"? Do you, from your own experience, agree with this? Why, or why not? Does the newspaper require more "direct participation" than radio or TV? Explain.

5. What is the importance of the idea on page 176 that "pictures lack tenses"? What points are made about magazines that distinguish them from books?

6. Do you regard commercials as "interruptors" of your TV viewing? of your radio listening? Why, or why not?

7. "Each medium selects its ideas." Think of all the differences you can among live theater, film, radio, and television. What is important about the actor in each? What is the role of the audience? Is one medium better at communicating something than the others? Which might be truer, for instance, to the reality of a forest fire? to the complexities of a divorce? to a description of trends in history? Why?

8. In reference to paragraph "6ix," has the appearance of TV made radio, the medium it replaced, more creative? What effect has TV had on movies?

9. McLuhan says of the new media that when they try to "usurp speech and personal, living relations, they harm." Where else in this book have you come across this view? Do you think Jerzy Kosinski would agree with McLuhan's views on books in paragraph "9ine"? Why, or why not?

Topic for Composition

1. Do some research on how the availability of media might have changed history. Would Paul Revere's ride have been necessary if telephones had existed? Would Martin Luther have nailed his 95 theses to the cathedral door if newspapers had existed?

Choose one historical event and one current event which involved a communication medium. Describe or dramatize how the historical event happened and how you think it would have happened if some modern medium had been available. Then, tell how the current event would be different without a particular medium.

The Media

Questions for Discussion

1. What exactly does Marshall McLuhan mean by "extension"? How is a wheel like a foot, for instance? What does a book do that an eye also does? How is a computer like our central nervous system? Do our inventions sometimes replace human activities? Do they improve upon them? If so, in what ways? What other things can you think of which are extensions of something human?

2. Look closely at the photographs on these pages. Notice the mouth of the tricycle rider, the texture of the girl's skin, the blurry speed of the electric circuitry (a pinball machine). What other qualities of these pictures can you comment on?

Topic for Composition

1. Select a simple idea which you would like to communicate, such as a proverb or saying, or perhaps one of McLuhan's statements, such as "TV is a tiny box into which people are crowded and must live," or "A new language lets us see with the fresh, sharp eyes of the child." Then decide upon a visual way to present the idea. The words must be included visibly somewhere. The form, however—poster, booklet, flip book, painting, collage, "soft sculpture"—is up to you. A well-thought-out idea is often not elaborate; try to "see" the point simply and effectively, perhaps using only lettering in a "new" form.

The City

Question for Discussion

1. Our inventions change us. We invented the city so that we could share and create a common culture. Television might be said to have replaced the city, since now through it we can share and create a common culture. Does television in an isolated shack change what the shack is? Would "hot coffee" on the desert change what a desert is? Would you say that all inventions are desirable since they change us? Why, or why not?

You Can See Why the Mighty Would Be Curious

Questions for Discussion

1. Howard Gossage is trying to clarify McLuhan's book, *Understanding Media,* in this essay. Do you feel that you understand McLuhan any better after reading this article? If so, in what ways?

2. If "medium" is defined as any extension of a human being, do all of our inventions then become media? Do they all tell us something about ourselves and the environment we have created? Try to think of some examples. For instance, what is a policeman an extension of? What function does a policeman amputate? What sense does a telephone extend? And so forth.

3. The senses extended by the most popular media at a given time determine the environment and the lives of the people at that time. A culture whose information is communicated by mouth and ear will have one kind of life. One in which people don't talk as much as they read will have another. What will be some of the possible differences between those two cultures?

4. A medium affects your life because you give it time, you stop doing things which you suddenly see as less important than that medium. Have you ever felt that you have chosen to spend time with a particular medium itself, rather than with the *content* of that medium? If so, explain. Which medium's "reality" is your favorite? Why?

5. In discussing the awareness that an old environment has become content for a newer one, Gossage explains that "either it changes or we do." What other examples can you think of to illustrate this change of awareness, besides the man who lost his leg or the man who drank martinis?

6. Think of some specific illustrations of the types of people described in this article as "extra-environmental." What can be the advantage of being "extra-environmental"? Have you ever been helped by someone who could view a situation with "fresher eyes" than yours? If so, in what way?

7. In talking about "a specialist's solution," the author says that "the odds are against its being a real answer." Why? Have you ever experienced or known about a problem with a specialist's solution, perhaps a mechanical or medical or environmental problem? If so, describe the difficulty. What are the implications of the last two sections of this essay for education and learning?

Topics for Composition

1. Read again the section on page 196 in which the author talks about environment changing without our noticing it, as in the example of travel. Think about ways in which your environment has changed during your own brief life. Has there been any recent environment that has changed for you that you were not aware of until reading this article and thinking about it? Write an essay describing one change in your environment and how you became aware of it.

2. Describe briefly a way in which reading this book has made any one of the mass media an "older environment" for you. In other words, have you stepped outside a plastic dome?

3. How do you react to McLuhan's ideas? Do you find them exciting? important? risky? fearful? hopeful? Are you one of those people mentioned in the final paragraph of Gossage's article? Write your reactions to McLuhan's thinking (and perhaps to the title of this article), now that you have nearly completed a chapter of his ideas.

Suppose He Is What He Sounds Like...

Questions for Discussion

1. Does Tom Wolfe's essay discuss some of the same points in McLuhan's philosophy as Howard Gossage's essay? Which ones? Do both writers have the same respect for McLuhan as a thinker?

2. Give some other examples, besides the dentist reducing pain with music, of how stepping up the intensity of one sense can force other senses to change intensity.

3. What, specifically, does Tom Wolfe mean when he says, "The electronic media . . . are causing an 'implosion' . . ."?

4. Do people in your neighborhood talk about places being "miles" or "minutes" away? Have you ever lived in a place, or do you remember a time, in which the other expression was used? If so, how were the two environments different?

5. "All anybody cares about is the time," Wolfe says in talking about travel. Collect airline ads for both foreign and domestic flights. Does Wolfe's statement prove true in the advertising?

6. On page 200, Wolfe describes TV children. Are you a product of the TV generation? Why, or why not? Do you consider yourself an aural or a visual (print) person? Are you satisfied with your relationship with people of the other part of society? Why, or why not?

7. In your own opinion, what if McLuhan *is* right? Do you think you would like the environment described in the last paragraph? Or don't you think you can judge that yet? Why, or why not?

8. The "construction" on page 198, *Coca Cola Plan* by Robert Rauschenberg, has elements that are surprising and incongruous—a rough, compartmented box; a blueprint; three Coke bottles; a pair of American eagle wings; and what else? Does America "fly" by the values put forth in Coca Cola's advertising?

9. The mural covering pages 200–203 is by James Rosenquist. What elements make it up? In what way does it interpret modern life? Is the tone of the mural critical? satirical? humorous? serious? In what way does this mural and the construction on page 198 say things that could not be said through language alone?

Topics for Composition

1. On page 201, the author gives an explanation for the drop-out rates in American schools today. Do you agree with his reasoning, or not? If you agree, write a paper making some concrete suggestions on what to do about the problem. If you disagree, write a specific paper telling why.

2. Write a fictional account about an encounter between an aural (tribal) and a visual (print) person. Tell it from the point of view of one or the other type of person, but not both. The encounter may be a conflict, a first experience, an observation, or a description of feelings. Try to make the narrator of the episode as true to the characteristics of the aural or the visual person as possible. You may set the story in past, present, or future time.

3. In the first chapter of this book, you wrote an interpretation of the phrase, "coping with the mass media." Have another look at what you wrote. Are your views any different now than they were then? Write an "updated" version of that essay, making any changes you feel are necessary.

ACKNOWLEDGMENTS

James Baldwin: For material from "Nothing Personal" by James Baldwin, from *Essays in Reflection,* edited by E. Graham Ward, Houghton Mifflin Company. Beacon Press: For selections from *Explorations in Communication,* edited by Edmund Carpenter and Marshall McLuhan; © 1960 by the Beacon Press. The Book Society of Canada: For material from *Servant or Master? A Casebook of Mass Media* by Max Braithwaite; copyright © The Book Society of Canada, Ltd., 1968; revised edition printed in Canada, 1972. Curtis Brown Ltd.: For "Reel One" by Adrien Stoutenburg, from *Mindscapes, Poems for the Real World,* edited by Richard Peck; copyright © 1964 by Adrien Stoutenburg. Farrar, Straus & Giroux, Inc.: For "Suppose he is what he sounds like, the most important thinker . . . ," from *The Pump House Gang* by Tom Wolfe; copyright 1968 by Tom Wolfe. Harcourt Brace Jovanovich, Inc.: For material from *How To Read Your Newspaper* by Ruth B. Smith and Barbara Michalak; copyright © 1970 by Harcourt Brace Jovanovich, Inc. For material from *Electric Media* by Les Brown in *Making Contact;* copyright © 1974 by Harcourt Brace Jovanovich, Inc. Harper & Row, Publishers, Inc.: For material abridged and adapted from "The Printed News System," in *The Information Machines* by Ben H. Bagdikian; copyright © 1971 by Rand Corporation. The Kiplinger Washington Editors, Inc.: For material from *Changing Times,* the Kiplinger Magazine, March, 1973; copyright 1973 by The Kiplinger Washington Editors, Inc. David and Marymae Klein: For material from *Supershopper, A Guide to Spending and Saving* by David and Marymae Klein. Little, Brown and Company: For material from *Going Steady* by Pauline Kael; copyright © 1968, 1969, 1970 by Pauline Kael. For selections from *How To Talk Back to Your Television Set* by Nicholas Johnson; copyright © 1967, 1968, 1969, 1970 by Little, Brown and Company. McIntosh and Otis, Inc.: For "How To Tell Good Guys from Bad Guys" by John Steinbeck; copyright © 1955 by John Steinbeck; originally appeared in *The Reporter.* Mad Magazine: For "The 'Late Show' Cliché Movie Scripts"; © 1970 by E. C. Publications, Inc. For "Interpreting the News"; © 1973 by E. C. Publications, Inc. National Advertising Review Board: For material from "Advertising Portraying or Directed to Women," from *Advertising Age.* Newsweek, Inc.: For material from "The New Movies"; copyright 1970 by Newsweek, Inc. For material from "The New Hollywood"; copyright 1974 by Newsweek, Inc.; reprinted by permission, all rights reserved. Parents' Magazine Press: For material from *Danger—Men Talking* by Stuart Chase; copyright 1969 by Stuart Chase. Ramparts Magazine, Inc.: For "You Can See Why the Mighty Would Be Curious" by Howard Luck Gossage; copyright 1966 by Ramparts Magazine, Inc.; reprinted by permission of the editors. Random House, Inc.: For "The Mass Media as 'Languages'," from *Man Must Speak* by Roy A. Gallant; copyright © 1968, 1969 by Roy A. Gallant. Saturday Review: For material from "Hollywood Lives" by the editors of *Saturday Review.* For "Hollywood's Mavericks" by Hollis Alpert. David Sohn and Jerzy Kosinski: For material from "A Nation of Videots: David Sohn Interviews Jerzy Kosinski"; original version first appeared in *Media and Methods,* April, 1975. Simon & Schuster, Inc.: For "The Camera and the Audience," from *The Public Arts* by Gilbert Seldes; copyright © 1956 by Gilbert Seldes. U. S. News & World Report: For material from "What TV Is Is Doing to America: An Interview with Alistair Cooke"; copyright 1974 by U. S. News & World Report, Inc.

ILLUSTRATION

William Seabright, cover; Herbert Loebel, 4; Allan D'Arcangelo, 10; Bill Owens from Magnum, 18; Patricia Hollander Gross from Stock, Boston, 25; Charles Harbutt from Magnum, 26, 124; Bruce Davidson from Magnum, 35; Courtesy of CBS, 36-37; Courtesy of NBC, 38; The Memory Shop, 42, 45, 50, 145, 149, 160, 167, 168-169; The Bettmann Archive, 46, 101; Movie Star News, 49, 53, 150, 156, 164, 165, 166; Lee Friedlander, 54; Ben Shahn, 59; Saul Steinberg, 64; Pictorial Parade, 68; Library of Congress, 73; Courtesy of *The Chicago Tribune,* 82, 95; Courtesy of *The New York Times,* 90-91; Culver Pictures, 104, 143, 148; Paul Hazelrigg, 116; John Mahtesian, 117-119; Burk Uzzle from Magnum, 120; Courtesy of the Museum of Modern Art/Film Stills Archive, 134, 155, 158-159, 163; Courtesy of United Artists Corporation, 140; Courtesy of Paramount Pictures, 146; Marshall F. Berman, Jr., 182-183, 184, 185, 186, 188-189; Wayne Sorce, 187; Edward Weston, 190; NASA, 192; Robert Rauschenberg, 198; Courtesy of Leo Castelli, 200-203.